LAYS OF THE WESTERN GAEL,

AND OTHER POEMS.

BY SAMUEL FERGUSON.

LONDON:

BELL AND DALDY, 186, FLEET STREET.

1865.

Library of Congress Cataloging in Publication Data

Ferguson, Samuel, Sir, 1810-1886.
    Lays of the western Gael, and other poems.

    Reprint of the 1865 ed. published by Bell and
Daldy, London.
    I. Title.
PR4699.F2L3 1978   821'.8   75-28813
ISBN 0-404-13806-3

Reprinted from the edition of 1865, London
First AMS edition published in 1978
Manufactured in the United States of America

AMS PRESS INC.
NEW YORK, N.Y.

LAYS OF THE WESTERN GAEL.

AMS PRESS

NEW YORK

CONTENTS.

THE TAIN-QUEST.

INTRODUCTORY NOTE.

HE *Tain*, in Irish Bardic phrase, was an heroic poem commemorative of a foray or plundering expedition on a grander scale. It was the duty of the bard to be prepared, at call, with all the principal *Tains*, among which the *Tain-Bo-Cuailgne*, or Cattle-Spoil of Quelny, occupied the first place ; as in it were recorded the exploits of all the personages most famous in the earlier heroic cycle of Irish story,—Conor Mac Nessa, Maev, Fergus Mac Roy, Conall Carnach, and Cuchullin.* Conor, King of Ulster, contemporary and rival of Maev, Queen of Connaught, reigned at Emania (now the Navan), near Armagh, about the commencement of the Christian era. He owed his first accession to the monarchy to the arts of his mother Nessa, on whom Fergus, his predecessor in the kingly office and step-father, doated so fondly that she had been enabled to stipulate, as a condition of bestowing her hand, that Fergus should abdicate for a year

---

* Pronounced *Ku-kullin.*

B

in favour of her youthful son. The year had been indefinitely prolonged by the fascinations of Nessa, aided by the ability of Conor, who, although he concealed a treacherous and cruel disposition under attractive graces of manners and person, ultimately became too popular to be displaced; and Fergus, whose nature disinclined him to the labours of government, had acquiesced in accepting as an equivalent the excitements of war and the chase, and the unrestricted pleasures of the revel. Associating with Cuchullin, Conall Carnach, Neesa son of Usnach, and the other companions of the military order of the Red Branch, he long remained a faithful supporter of the throne of his stepson, eminent for his valour, generosity, and fidelity, as well as for his accomplishments as a hunter and a poet.

At length occurred the tragedy which broke up these genial associations, and drove Fergus into the exile in which he died. Deirdra, a beautiful virgin, educated by Conor for his own companionship, saw and loved Neesa, who eloped with her, and dreading the wrath of the king, fled to Scotland, accompanied by his brothers and clansmen. Conor contemplating the treachery he afterwards practised, acquiesced in the entreaty of his councillors that the sons of Usnach should be pardoned and restored to the service of their country; and to Fergus was confided the task of discovering their retreat and escorting them to Emania under security of safe-conduct. The hunting-cry of Fergus was heard and recognized by the exiles where they lay in green booths in the solitude of Glen Etive. On their return to Ireland, a temptation prepared for the simple-minded convivial Fergus detached him from his wards; and Deirdra and the clan Usnach proceeded under the guardianship of his sons, Buino and Illan, to Emania. Here they were lodged in the house of the Red Branch, where, although it soon became apparent that Conor intended their destruction, they repressed all appearance of distrust in their protectors, and calmly continued playing chess until, Buino having been bought over, and Illan slain in their defence, they were at length compelled to salley from the burning edifice, and were put to the sword; Deirdra being seized again into the king's possession. On this atrocious outrage Fergus took up arms as well to regain his crown as to avenge the abuse of his safe-conduct; but Cuchullin and the principal chiefs remaining faithful to Conor, the much injured ex-king betook himself with others of the disgusted Ultonian nobles to the protection of Maev and Ailill, the Queen and King consort of Connaught. Thus strengthened, the warriors of Maev made frequent incursions into the territories of Conor, in which Keth and Beälcu on the one hand, and Cuchullin and Conall Carnach on the other, were the most renowned actors. After many years of desultory warfare, a pretext for the invasion of the rich plain of Louth arose in consequence of a chief of the territory of Cuailgne having ill-treated the messengers of Maev, sent by her to negociate the purchase of a notable dun bull, and the great expedition was thereupon organized which forms

the subject of the *Tain-Bo-Cuailgne.* The guidance of
the invading host, which traversed the counties of Ros-
common, Longford and Westmeath, was at first confided
to Fergus; and much of the interest of the story turns on
the conflict in his breast between his duty towards his
adopted sovereign, and his attachment to his old com-
panions in arms and former subjects. On the borders
of Cuailgne the invaders were encountered by Cuchullin,
who alone detained them by successive challenges to
single combat, until Conor and the Ultonian chiefs were
enabled to assemble their forces. In these encounters
Cuchullin also had the pain of combatting former com-
panions and fellow-pupils in arms; among others, Fer-
dia, who had received his military education at the same
school and under the same amazonian instructress at
Dun Sciah, in view of the Cuchullin hills, in Skye. In
the respites of their combat the heroes kiss in memory
of their early affection. The name of the ford in which
they fought (*Ath-Firdiadh*, now Ardee in the county of
Louth) perpetuates the memory of the fallen champion,
and helps to fix the locality of these heroic passages.
Maev, though ultimately overthrown at the great battle of
Slewin in Westmeath, succeeded in carrying off the spoils
of Louth, including the dun bull of Cuailgne; and with
Fergus, under the shelter of whose shield she effected
her retreat through many sufferings and dangers, re-
turned to Croghan, the Connacian royal residence, near
Elphin in Roscommon. Here she bore to the now
aged hero (at a birth, says the story) three sons, from

whom three of the great native families still trace their descent, and from the eldest of whom the county of Kerry derives its name. A servant of Ailill, at the command of the king, avenged the injury done his master's bed by piercing Fergus with a spear, while the athlete poet swam, defenceless, bathing in Loch Ein. The earliest copies of the *Tain-Bo-Cuailgne* are prefaced by the wild legend of its loss and recovery in the time of Guary, King of Connaught, in the sixth century, by Murgen, son of the chief poet Sanchan, under circumstances which have suggested the following poem. The Ogham characters referred to in the piece, were formed by lines cut tally-wise on the corners of stone pillars, and somewhat resembled Scandinavian Runes, examples of which, carved on squared staves, may still be seen in several museums. The readers of the *Tain-Bo-Cuailgne,* as it now exists, have to regret the overlaying of much of its heroic and pathetic material by turgid extravagances and exaggerations, the additions apparently of later copyists.

THE TAIN-QUEST.

BEAR the cup to Sanchan Torpest; yield
the bard his poet's meed;
What we've heard was but a foretaste;
lays more lofty now succeed.

Though my stores be emptied well-nigh, twin bright
cups there yet remain,—

Win them with the Raid of Cuailgne; chaunt us,
Bard, the famous *Tain!*"

Thus, in hall of Gort, spake Guary; for the king,
let truth be told,

Bounteous though he was, was weary giving goblets,
giving gold,

Giving aught the bard demanded;[1] but, when for
the *Tain* he call'd,

Sanchan from his seat descended; shame and anger
fired the Scald.

" Well," he said, " 'tis known through Erin, known
    through Alba, main and coast,

Since the Staff-Book's disappearing over sea, the
    Tain is lost:

For the lay was cut in tallies on the corners of the
    staves

Patrick in his pilgrim galleys carried o'er the Ictian
    waves.

" Well 'tis known that Erin's Ollaves, met in Tara
    Luachra's hall,[2]

Fail'd to find the certain knowledge of the *Tain*
    amongst them all,

Though there there sat sages hoary, men who in
    their day had known

All the foremost kings of story; but the lay was
    lost and gone.

" Wherefore from that fruitless session went I forth
    myself in quest

Of the *Tain;* nor intermission, even for hours of
    needful rest,

Gave I to my sleepless searches, till I Erin, hill
    and plain,

Courts and castles, cells and churches, roam'd and
    ransack'd, but in vain.

" Dreading shame on bardship branded, should I
    e'er be put to own
Any lay of right demanded of me was not rightly
    known,
Over sea to Alba sped I, where, amid the hither
    Gael,[3]
Dalriad bards had fill'd already all Cantyre with
    song and tale.

" Who the friths and fords shall reckon; who the
    steeps I cross'd shall count,
From the cauldron-pool of Brecan eastward o'er the
    Alban mount;[4]
From the stone fort of Dun Britan, set o'er circling
    Clyde on high,[5]
Northward to the thunder-smitten, jagg'd Cuchullin
    peaks of Skye?

" Great Cuchullin's name and glory fill'd the land
    from north to south;
Deirdra's and Clan Usnach's story rife I found in
    every mouth;

Yea, and where the whitening surges spread below
    the Herdsman Hill,[6]
Echoes of the shout of Fergus haunted all Glen
    Etive still.

" Echoes of the shout of warning heard by Usnach's
    exiled youths,
When, between the night and morning, sleeping in
    their hunting booths,
Deirdra dreamt the death-bird hooted; Neesa, wak-
    ing wild with joy,
Cried, ' A man of Erin shouted! welcome Fergus,
    son of Roy !'

" Wondrous shout, from whence repeated, even as
    up the answering hills
Echo's widening wave proceeded, spreads the sound
    of song that fills
All the echoing waste of ages, tale and lay and
    choral strain,
But the chief delight of sages and of kings was still
    the *Tain*,

" Made when mighty Maev invaded Cuailgnia for
    her brown-bright bull;

Fergus was the man that made it, for he saw the
　　　　war in full,
And in Maev's own chariot mounted, sang what
　　　　pass'd before his eyes,
As you'd hear it now recounted, knew I but where
　　　　Fergus lies.

" Bear me witness, Giant Bouchaill, herdsman of
　　　　the mountain drove,
How with spell and spirit-struggle many a midnight
　　　　hour I strove
Back to life to call the author ! for before I'd hear
　　　　it said,
' Neither Sanchan knew it,' rather would I learn it
　　　　from the dead ;

" Ay, and pay the dead their teaching with the one
　　　　price spirits crave,
When the hand of magic, reaching past the barriers
　　　　of the grave,
Drags the struggling phantom lifeward :—but the
　　　　Ogham on his stone
Still must mock us undecipher'd ; grave and lay
　　　　alike unknown.

" So that put to shame the direst, here I stand and
  own, O King,

Thou a lawful lay requirest Sanchan Torpest cannot
  sing.

Take again the gawds you gave me,—cup nor
  crown no more will I ;—

Son, from further insult save me : lead me hence,
  and let me die."

Leaning on young Murgen's shoulder—Murgen
  was his youngest son—

Jeer'd of many a lewd beholder, Sanchan from the
  hall has gone :

But, when now beyond Loch Lurgan, three days
  thence he reach'd his home,[7]

"Give thy blessing, Sire," said Murgen.—"Whither
  wouldst thou, son ?"—" To Rome ;

" Rome, or, haply, Tours of Martin ; wheresoever
  over ground

Hope can deem that tidings certain of the lay may
  yet be found."

Answered Eimena his brother, " Not alone thou
  leav'st the west,

Though thou ne'er shouldst find another, I'll be
    comrade of the quest."

Eastward, breadthwise, over Erin straightway tra-
    vell'd forth the twain,
Till with many days' wayfaring Murgen fainted by
    Loch Ein:
" Dear my brother, thou art weary: I for present
    aid am flown;
Thou for my returning tarry here beside this Stand-
    ing Stone."

Shone the sunset, red and solemn: Murgen, where
    he leant, observed
Down the corners of the column letter-strokes of
    Ogham carved.
" 'Tis, belike, a burial pillar," said he, " and these
    shallow lines
Hold some warrior's name of valour, could I rightly
    spell the signs."

Letter then by letter tracing, soft he breathed the
    sound of each;
Sound and sound then interlacing, lo, the signs
    took form of speech;

And with joy and wonder mainly thrilling, part
a-thrill with fear,
Murgen read the legend plainly, " FERGUS, SON
OF ROY IS HERE."

" Lo," said he, " my quest is ended, knew I but
the spell to say;
Underneath my feet extended, lies the man that
made the lay :
Yet, though spell nor incantation know I, were the
words but said
That could speak my soul's elation, I, methinks,
could raise the dead.

" Be an arch-bard's name my warrant.   Murgen,
son of Sanchan, here,
Vow'd upon a venturous errand to the door-sills of
Saint Pierre,
Where, beyond Slieve Alpa's barrier, sits the Coärb
of the keys,[8]
I conjure thee, buried warrior, rise and give my
wanderings 'ease.

" 'Tis not death whose forms appalling strew the
steep with pilgrim's graves,

'Tis not fear of snow-slips falling, nor of ice-clefts'
    azure caves
Daunts me; but I dread if Romeward I must travel
    till the *Tain*
Crowns my quest, these footsteps homeward I shall
    never turn again.

" I at parting left behind me aged sire and mother
    dear;
Who a parent's love shall find me ere again I ask
    it here?
Dearer too than sire or mother, ah, how dear these
    tears may tell,
I, at parting, left another; left a maid who loves
    me well.

" Ruthful clay, thy rigours soften! Fergus, hear,
    thy deaf heaps through,
Thou, thyself a lover often, aid a lover young and
    true !
Thou, the favourite of maidens, for a fair young
    maiden's sake,
I conjure thee by the radiance of thy Nessa's eyes,
    awake !

" Needs there adjuration stronger? Fergus, thou
      hadst once a son :
Even than I was Illan younger when the glorious
      feat was done,—
When in hall of Red Branch biding Deirdra and
      Clan Usnach sate,
In thy guarantee confiding, though the foe was at
      their gate.

" Though their guards were bribed and flying, and
      their door-posts wrapp'd in flame,
Calmly on thy word relying bent they o'er the
      chessman game,
Till with keen words sharp and grievous Deirdra
      cried through smoke and fire,
' See the sons of Fergus leave us : traitor sons of
      traitor sire !'

" Mild the eyes that did upbraid her, when young
      Illan rose and spake,
' If my father be a traitor; if my brother for the
      sake
Of a bribe bewray his virtue, yet while lives the
      sword I hold,

Illan Finn will not desert you, not for fire and not
    for gold !'

" And as hawk that strikes on pigeons, sped on
    wrath's unswerving wing
Through the tyrant's leaguering legions, smiting
    chief and smiting king,
Smote he full on Conor's gorget, till the waves of
    welded steel
Round the monarch's magic target rang their loudest
    larum peal.

" Rang the disc where wizard hammers, mingling
    in the wavy field,
Tempest-wail and breaker-clamours, forged the won-
    drous Ocean shield,
Answering to whose stormy noises, oft as clang'd
    by deadly blows,
All the echoing kindred voices of the seas of Erin
    rose.

" Moan'd each sea-chafed promontory; soar'd and
    wail'd white Cleena's wave; [9]
Rose the Tonn of Inver Rory, and through column'd
    chasm and cave

Reaching deep with roll of anger, till Dunseverick's
      dungeons reel'd,
Roar'd responsive to the clangour struck from
      Conor's magic shield.

" Ye, remember, red wine quaffing in Dunseverick's
      halls of glee,
Heard the moaning, heard the chafing, heard the
      thundering from the sea;
Knew that peril compass'd Conor, came, and on
      Emania's plain
Found his fraud and thy dishonour; Deirdra
      ravish'd, Illan slain.

" Now, by love of son for father,—son, who ere he'd
      hear it said—
' Neither Sanchan knew it,' rather seeks to learn it
      from the dead;
Rise, and give me back the story that the twin gold
      cups shall win;
Rise, recount the great Cow-Foray! rise for love of
      Illan Finn!

" Still he stirs not.   Love of woman thou regard'st
      not Fergus, now:

Love of children, instincts human, care for these
      no more hast thou :
Wider comprehensions, deeper insights to the dead
      belong :—
Since for Love thou wakest not, sleeper, yet awake
      for sake of Song !

" Thou, the first in rhythmic cadence dressing life's
      discordant tale,
Wars of chiefs and loves of maidens, gavest the
      Poem to the Gael ;
Now they've lost their noblest measure, and in
      dark days hard at hand,
Song shall be the only treasure left them in their
      native land.

" Not for selfish gawds or baubles dares my soul
      disturb the graves :
Love consoles, but song ennobles ; songless men are
      meet for slaves :
Fergus, for the Gael's sake, waken ! never let the
      scornful Gauls
'Mongst our land's reproaches reckon lack of Song
      within our halls ! "

Fergus rose. A mist ascended with him, and a flash
      was seen
As of brazen sandals blended with a mantle's wafture
      green;
But so thick the cloud closed o'er him, Eimena,
      return'd at last,
Found not on the field before him but a mist-heap
      grey and vast.

Thrice to pierce the hoar recesses faithful Eimena
      essay'd;
Thrice through foggy wildernesses back to open air
      he stray'd;
Till a deep voice through the vapours fill'd the twi-
      light far and near,
And the Night her starry tapers kindling, stoop'd
      from heaven to hear.

Seem'd as though the skiey Shepherd back to earth
      had cast the fleece
Envying gods of old caught upward from the dark-
      ening shrines of Greece;
So the white mists curl'd and glisten'd, so from
      heaven's expanses bare,

Stars enlarging lean'd and listen'd down the emptied
    depths of air.

All night long by mists surrounded Murgen lay in
    vapoury bars;
All night long the deep voice sounded 'neath the
    keen, enlarging stars:
But when, on the orient verges, stars grew dim and
    mists retired,
Rising by the stone of Fergus, Murgen stood, a man
    inspired.

" Back to Sanchan!—Father, hasten, ere the hour of
    power be past,
Ask not how obtain'd, but listen to the lost lay
    found at last!"
" Yea, these words have tramp of heroes in them;
    and the marching rhyme
Rolls the voices of the Era's down the echoing
    steeps of Time."

Not till all was thrice related, thrice recital full
    essay'd,
Sad and shame-faced, worn and faded, Murgen
    sought the faithful maid.

" Ah, so haggard; ah, so altered; thou in life and
  love so strong !"

" Dearly purchased," Murgen falter'd, " life and
  love I've sold for song !"

" Woe is me, the losing bargain ! what can song
  the dead avail ?"

" Fame immortal," murmur'd Murgen, " long as
  lay delights the Gael."

" Fame, alas ! the price thou chargest not repays
  one virgin tear."

" Yet the proud revenge I've purchased for my sire,
  I deem not dear."

So, again to Gort the splendid, when the drinking
  boards were spread,

Sanchan, as of old attended, came and sat at table-
  head.

" Bear the cup to Sanchan Torpest: twin gold
  goblets, Bard, are thine,

If with voice and string thou harpest, *Tain-Bo-
  Cuailgne*, line for line."

" Yea, with voice and string I'll chant it." Murgen
  to his father's knee

Set the harp: no prelude wanted, Sanchan struck
    the master key,
And, as bursts the brimful river all at once from
    caves of Cong,
Forth at once, and once for ever, leap'd the torrent
    of the song.

Floating on a brimful torrent, men go down and
    banks go by:
Caught adown the lyric current, Guary, captured,
    ear and eye,
Heard no more the courtiers jeering, saw no more
    the walls of Gort,
Creeve Roe's meads instead appearing, and Emania's
    royal fort.

Vision chasing splendid vision, Sanchan roll'd the
    rhythmic scene;
They that mock'd in lewd derision now, at gaze,
    with wondering mien,
Sate, and, as the glorying master sway'd the tight-
    ening reins of song,
Felt emotion's pulses faster—fancies faster bound
    along.

Pity dawn'd on savage faces, when for love of cap-
  tive Crunn,
Macha, in the ransom-races, girt her gravid loins,
  to run [10]
'Gainst the fleet Ultonian horses; and, when Deirdra
  on the road
Headlong dash'd her 'mid the corses, brimming
  eyelids overflow'd.

Light of manhood's generous ardour, under brows
  relaxing shone;
When, mid-ford, on Uladh's border, young Cu-
  chullin stood alone,
Maev and all her hosts withstanding:—" Now, for
  love of knightly play,
Yield the youth his soul's demanding; let the hosts
  their marchings stay,

" Till the death he craves be given; and, upon his
  burial stone
Champion-praises duly graven, make his name and
  glory known;
For, in speech-containing token, age to ages never
  gave

Salutation better spoken, than, ' Behold a hero's
grave.' "

What, another and another, and he still for combat
calls ?
Ah, the lot on thee, his brother sworn in arms,
Ferdia, falls ;
And the hall with wild applauses sobb'd like women
ere they wist,
When the champions in the pauses of the deadly
combat kiss'd.

Now, for love of land and cattle, while Cuchullin
in the fords
Stays the march of Connaught's battle, ride and
rouse the Northern Lords ;
Swift as angry eagles wing them toward the plun-
der'd eyrie's call,
Thronging from Dun Dealga[11] bring them, bring
them from the Red Branch hall !

Heard ye not the tramp of armies ? Hark ! amid the
sudden gloom,
'Twas the stroke of Conall's war-mace sounded
through the startled room ;

And, while still the hall grew darker, king and
    courtier chill'd with dread,
Heard the rattling of the war-car of Cuchullin over-
    head.

Half in wonder, half in terror, loth to stay and loth
    to fly,
Seem'd to each beglamour'd hearer shades of kings
    went thronging by :
But the troubled joy of wonder merged at last in
    mastering fear,
As they heard, through pealing thunder, " Fergus,
    son of Roy is here!"

Brazen-sandall'd, vapour-shrouded, moving in an
    icy blast,
Through the doorway terror-crowded, up the tables
    Fergus pass'd :—
" Stay thy hand, oh harper, pardon! cease the
    wild unearthly lay !
Murgen, bear thy sire his guerdon." Murgen sat,
    a shape of clay.

' Bear him on his bier beside me : never more in
    halls of Gort

Shall a niggard king deride me ; slaves, of Sanchan
    make their sport !
But because the maiden's yearnings needs must also
    be condoled,
Hers shall be the dear-bought earnings, hers the
    twin-bright cups of gold."

" Cups," she cried, " of bitter drinking, fling them
    far as arm can throw !
Let them, in the ocean sinking, out of sight and
    memory go !
Let the joinings of the rhythm, let the links of sense
    and sound
Of the *Tain-Bo* perish with them, lost as though
    they'd ne'er been found !"

So it comes, the lay, recover'd once at such a deadly
    cost,
Ere one full recital suffer'd, once again is all but
    lost :
For, the maiden's malediction still with many a
    blemish-stain
Clings in coarser garb of fiction round the fragments
    that remain.

THE ABDICATION OF FERGUS

MAC ROY.

ONCE, ere God was crucified,
 I was King o'er Uladh wide:
 King, by law of choice and birth,
O'er the fairest realm of Earth.

I was head of Rury's race;
Emain was my dwelling-place;[12]
Right and Might were mine; nor less
Stature, strength, and comeliness.

Neither lack'd I love's delight,
Nor the glorious meeds of fight.
All on earth was mine could bring
Life's enjoyment to a king.

Much I loved the jocund chase,
Much the horse and chariot race:
Much I loved the deep carouse,
Quaffing in the Red Branch House.[13]

But, in Council call'd to meet,
Loved I not the judgment seat;
And the suitors' questions hard
Won but scantly my regard.

Rather would I, all alone,
Care and state behind me thrown,
Walk the dew through showery gleams
O'er the meads, or by the streams,

Chanting, as the thoughts might rise,
Unimagined melodies;
While with sweetly-pungent smart
Secret happy tears would start.

Such was I, when, in the dance,
Nessa did bestow a glance,
And my soul that moment took
Captive in a single look.

I am but an empty shade,
Far from life and passion laid;
Yet does sweet remembrance thrill
All my shadowy being still.

Nessa had been Fathna's spouse,
Fathna of the Royal house,
And a beauteous boy had borne him;
Fourteen summers did adorn him:

Yea; thou deem'st it marvellous,
That a widow's glance should thus
Turn from lure of maidens' eyes
All a young king's fantasies.

Yet if thou hadst known but half
Of the joyance of her laugh,
Of the measures of her walk,
Of the music of her talk,

Of the witch'ry of her wit,
Even when smarting under it,—
Half the sense, the charm, the grace,
Thou hadst worshipp'd in my place.

And, besides, the thoughts I wove
Into songs of war and love,
She alone of all the rest
Felt them with a perfect zest.

" Lady, in thy smiles to live
Tell me but the boon to give,
Yea, I lay in gift complete
Crown and sceptre at thy feet."

" Not so great the boon I crave :
Hear the wish my soul would have ;"
And she glanc'd a loving eye
On the stripling standing by :—

" Conor is of age to learn ;
Wisdom is a king's concern ;
Conor is of royal race,
Yet may sit in Fathna's place.

" Therefore, king, if thou wouldst prove
That I have indeed thy love,
On the judgment-seat permit
Conor by thy side to sit,

" That by use the youth may draw
Needful knowledge of the Law."
I with answer was not slow,
" Be thou mine, and be it so."

I am but a shape of air,
Far removed from love's repair;
Yet, were mine a living frame
Once again I'd say the same.

Thus, a prosperous wooing sped,
Took I Nessa to my bed,
While in council and debate
Conor daily by me sate.

Modest was his mien in sooth,
Beautiful the studious youth,
Questioning with earnest gaze
All the reasons and the ways

In the which, and why because,
Kings administer the Laws.
Silent so with looks intent
Sat he till the year was spent.

But the strifes the suitors raised
Bred me daily more distaste,
Every faculty and passion
Sunk in sweet intoxication.

Till upon a day in court
Rose a plea of weightier sort:
Tangled as a briary thicket
Were the rights and wrongs intricate

Which the litigants disputed,
Challenged, mooted, and confuted;
Till, when all the plea was ended,
Naught at all I comprehended.

Scorning an affected show
Of the thing I did not know,
Yet my own defect to hide,
I said " Boy-judge, thou decide."

Conor, with unalter'd mien,
In a clear sweet voice serene,
Took in hand the tangled skein
And began to make it plain.

As a sheep-dog sorts his cattle,
As a king arrays his battle,
So, the facts on either side
He did marshal and divide.

Every branching side-dispute
Traced he downward to the root
Of the strife's main stem, and there
Laid the ground of difference bare.

Then to scope of either cause
Set the compass of the laws,
This adopting, that rejecting,—
Reasons to a head collecting,—

As a charging cohort goes
Through and over scatter'd foes,
So, from point to point, he brought
Onward still the weight of thought

Through all error and confusion,
Till he set the clear conclusion
Standing like a king alone,
All things adverse overthrown,

D

And gave judgment clear and sound:—
Praises fill'd the hall around;
Yea, the man that lost the cause
Hardly could withhold applause.

By the wondering crowd surrounded
I sat shamefaced and confounded.
Envious ire awhile oppress'd me
Till the nobler thought possess'd me;

And I rose, and on my feet
Standing by the judgment-seat,
Took the circlet from my head,
Laid it on the bench, and said,

" Men of Uladh, I resign
That which is not rightly mine,
That a worthier than I
May your judge's place supply.

" Lo, it is no easy thing
For a man to be a king
Judging well, as should behove
One who claims a people's love.

" Uladh's judgment-seat to fill
I have neither wit nor will.
One is here may justly claim
Both the function and the name.

" Conor is of royal blood;
Fair he is; I trust him good;
Wise he is we all may say
Who have heard his words to-day.

" Take him therefore in my room,
Letting me the place assume—
Office but with life to end—
Of his councillor and friend."

So young Conor gain'd the crown;
So I laid the kingship down;
Laying with it as it went
All I knew of discontent.

THE HEALING OF CONALL CARNACH.

INTRODUCTORY NOTE.

CONOR is said to have heard of the Passion of our Lord from a Roman captain sent to demand tribute at Emania. He died of a wound inflicted by Keth, son of Magach, and nephew of Maev, with a ball from a sling; having been inveigled within reach of the missile by certain Connaught ladies. His son Forbaid characteristically avenged his death by the assassination of Maev, whom he slew, also with a sling, across the Shannon, while she was in the act of bathing. Notwithstanding the repulsive character of many of the acts ascribed to Conor, such as the cruel enforcement of the foot-race upon Macha (*O licentiam furoris, ægræ reipublicæ gemitu prosequendam!*)* and the betrayal of the sons of Usnach, and abduction of Deirdra, the best part of Irish heroic tradition connects itself with his reign and period, pre-

---

* VAL. MAX. lib. ix. *De Improb. dict. et fact.*

ceding by nearly three centuries the epoch of Cormac
Mac Art, and the Fenian or Irish Ossianic romances.
The survivor of the men of renown of Conor's era was
Conall Carnach, the hero of many picturesque legends,
one of the most remarkable of which affords the ground-
work for the following verses.

THE HEALING OF CONALL CARNACH.

'ER Slieve Few,[14] with noiseless tramping
    through the heavy-drifted snow,
    Beälcu,* Connacia's champion, in his
    chariot tracks the foe;
And anon far off discerneth, in the mountain-hollow
    white,
Slinger Keth and Conall Carnach mingling, hand
    to hand, in fight.

Swift the charioteer his coursers urged across the
    wintry glade:
Hoarse the cry of Keth and hoarser seem'd to come
    demanding aid;

---

* Pronounced *Bayal-kú.*.

But through wreath and swollen runnel ere the car
    could reach anigh,
Keth lay dead, and mighty Conall bleeding lay at
    point to die.

Whom beholding spent and pallid, Beälcu exulting
    cried,
" Oh thou ravening wolf of Uladh, where is now
    thy northern pride ?
What can now that crest audacious, what that pale
    defiant brow,
Once the bale-star of Connacia's ravaged fields, avail
    thee now ?"

" Taunts are for reviling women ;" faintly Conall
    made reply :
" Wouldst thou play the manlier foeman, end my
    pain and let me die.
Neither deem thy blade dishonour'd that with Keth's
    a deed it share,
For the foremost two of Connaught feat enough and
    fame to spare."

" No, I will not ! bard shall never in Dunseverick
    hall make boast

That to quell one northern riever needed two of
    Croghan's host.[15]

But because that word thou'st spoken, if but life
    enough remains,

Thou shalt hear the wives of Croghan clap their
    hands above thy chains.

" Yea, if life enough but linger, that the leech may
    make thee whole,

Meet to satiate the anger that beseems a warrior's
    soul,

Best of leech-craft I'll purvey thee; make thee whole
    as healing can;

And in single combat slay thee, Connaught man to
    Ulster man."

Binding him in five-fold fetter,[16] wrists and ankles,
    wrists and neck,

To his car's uneasy litter Beälcu upheaved the
    wreck

Of the broken man and harness; but he started with
    amaze

When he felt the northern war-mace, what a weight
    it was to raise.

Westward then through Breiffny's borders, with
      his captive and his dead,
Track'd by bands of fierce applauders, wives and
      shrieking widows, sped;
And the chain'd heroic carcass on the fair-green of
      Moy Slaught [17]
Casting down, proclaim'd his purpose, and bade
      Lee the leech be brought.

Lee, the gentle-faced physician from his herb-plot
      came, and said,
" Healing is with God's permission: health for
      life's enjoyment made:
And though I mine aid refuse not, yet, to speak
      my purpose plain,
I the healing art abuse not, making life enure to
      pain.

" But assure me, with the sanction of the mightiest
      oath ye know,
That in case, in this contention, Conall overcome
      his foe,
Straight departing from the tourney by what path
      the chief shall choose,

He is free to take his journey unmolested to the
   Fews.

" Swear me further, while at healing in my charge
   the hero lies,
None shall through my fences stealing, work him
   mischief or surprise;
So, if God the undertaking but approve, in six
   months' span
Once again my art shall make him meet to stand
   before a man."

Crom their god they then attested, Sun and Wind
   for guarantees,
Conall Carnach unmolested by what exit he might
   please,
If the victor, should have freedom to depart Con-
   nacia's bounds;
Meantime, no man should intrude him, entering on
   the hospice grounds.

Then his burthen huge receiving in the hospice-
   portal, Lee,
Stiffen'd limb by limb relieving with the iron fetter
   key,

As a crumpled scroll unroll'd him, groaning deep,
    till laid at length,
Wondering gazers might behold him, what a tower
    he was of strength.

Spake the sons to one another, day by day, of
    Beälcu—
" Get thee up and spy, my brother, what the leech
    and northman do."
" Lee, at mixing of a potion: Conall, yet in no wise
    dead,
As on reef of rock the ocean, tosses wildly on his
    bed."

" Spy again with cautious peeping: what of Lee
    and Conall now?"
" Conall lies profoundly sleeping: Lee beside with
    placid brow."
" And to-day?" " To-day he's risen; pallid as his
    swathing sheet,
He has left his chamber's prison, and is walking on
    his feet."

" And to-day?" " A ghastly figure, on his javelin
    propp'd he goes."

" And to-day?" " A languid vigour through his
  larger gesture shows."
" And to-day?" " The blood renewing mantles all
  his clear cheek through."
" Would thy vow had room for rueing, rashly-
  valiant Beälcu!"

So with herb and healing balsam, ere the second
  month was past,
Life's additions smooth and wholesome circling
  through his members vast,
As you've seen a sere oak burgeon under summer
  showers and dew,
Conall, under his chirurgeon, fill'd and flourish'd,
  spread and grew.

" I can bear the sight no longer: I have watch'd
  him moon by moon:
Day by day the chief grows stronger: giant-strong
  he will be soon.
Oh my sire, rash-valiant warrior! but that oaths
  have built the wall,
Soon these feet should leap the barrier: soon this
  hand thy fate forestall."

" Brother, have the wish thou'st utter'd: we have
     sworn, so let it be;
But although our feet be fetter'd, all the air is left
     us free.
Dying Keth with vengeful presage did bequeath thee
     sling and ball,
And the sling may send its message where thy
     vagrant glances fall.

" Forbaid was a master-slinger: Maev, when in her
     bath she sank,
Felt the presence of his finger from the further
     Shannon bank;
For he threw by line and measure, practising a con-
     stant cast
Daily in secluded leisure, till he reach'd the mark
     at last.[18]

" Keth achieved a warrior's honour, though 'twas
     mid a woman's band,
When he smote the amorous Conor bowing from
     his distant stand.[19]
Fit occasion will not fail ye: in the leech's lawn
     below,

Conall at the fountain daily drinks within an easy
  throw."

" Wherefore cast ye at the apple, sons of mine, with
  measured aim ?"
" He who in the close would grapple, first the distant
  foe should maim.
And since Keth, his death-balls casting, rides no
  more the ridge of war,
We, against our summer hosting, train us for his
  vacant car."

" Wherefore to the rock repairing, gaze ye forth,
  my children, tell."
" 'Tis a stag we watch for snaring, that frequents
  the leech's well."
" I will see this stag, though, truly, small may be
  my eyes delight."
And he climb'd the rock where fully lay the lawn
  exposed to sight.

Conall to the green well-margin came at dawn and
  knelt to drink,
Thinking how a noble virgin by a like green
  fountain's brink

Heard his own pure vows one morning, far away
    and long ago :
All his heart to home was turning ; and his tears
    began to flow.

Clean forgetful of his prison, steep Dunseverick's
    windy tower
Seem'd to rise in present vision, and his own dear
    lady's bower.
Round the sheltering knees they gather, little ones
    of tender years,—
Tell us mother of our father—and she answers but
    with tears.

Twice the big drops plash'd the fountain.   Then he
    rose, and, turning round,
As across a breast of mountain sweeps a whirlwind,
    o'er the ground
Raced in athlete-feats amazing, swung the war-mace,
    hurl'd the spear ;
Beälcu, in wonder gazing, felt the pangs of deadly
    fear.

Had it been a fabled griffin, suppled in a fasting
    den,

Flash'd its wheeling coils to heaven o'er a wreck of
      beasts and men,
Hardly had the dreadful prospect bred his soul
      more dire alarms;
Such the fire of Conall's aspect, such the stridor of
      his arms !

" This is fear," he said, " that never shook these
      limbs of mine till now.
Now I see the mad endeavour; now I mourn the
      boastful vow.
Yet 'twas righteous wrath impell'd me; and a sense
      of manly shame
From his naked throat withheld me when 'twas
      offer'd to my aim.

" Now I see his strength excelling: whence he
      buys it: what he pays :
'Tis a God who has his dwelling in the fount, to
      whom he prays.
Thither came he weeping, drooping, till the Well-
      God heard his prayer :
Now behold him, soaring, swooping, as an eagle
      through the air.

" O thou God, by whatsoever sounds of awe thy
    name we know,
Grant thy servant equal favour with the stranger
    and the foe !
Equal grace, 'tis all I covet; and if sacrificial blood
Win thy favour, thou shalt have it on thy very
    well-brink, God !

" What and though I've given pledges not to cross
    the leech's court ?
Not to pass his sheltering hedges, meant I to his
    patient's hurt.
Thy dishonour meant I never: never meant I to
    forswear
Right divine of prayer wherever Power divine
    invites to prayer.

" Sun that warm'st me, Wind that fann'st me, ye
    that guarantee the oath,
Make no sign of wrath against me: tenderly ye
    touch me both.
Yea, then, through his fences stealing ere to-morrow's
    sun shall rise,

Well-God! on thy margin kneeling, I will offer
　　　sacrifice."

" Brother, rise, the skies grow ruddy : if we yet
　　　would save our sire,
Rests a deed courageous, bloody, wondering ages
　　　shall admire :
Hie thee to the spy-rock's summit : ready there
　　　thou'lt find the sling ;
Ready there the leaden plummet; and at dawn he
　　　seeks the spring."

Ruddy dawn had changed to amber : radiant as the
　　　yellow day,
Conall, issuing from his chamber, to the fountain
　　　took his way :
There, athwart the welling water, like a fallen pillar,
　　　spread,
Smitten by the bolt of slaughter, lay Connacia's
　　　champion dead.

Call the hosts ! convene the judges ! cite the dead
　　　man's children both !—
Said the judges, " He gave pledges ; Sun and
　　　Wind ; and broke the oath,

And they slew him: so we've written: let his sons
    attend our words."
" Both, by sudden frenzy smitten, fell at sunrise on
    their swords."

Then the judges, " Ye who punish man's pre-
    varicating vow,
Needs not further to admonish: contrite to your
    will we bow,
All our points of promise keeping: safely let the
    chief go forth."
Conall to his chariot leaping, turned his coursers to
    the north :

In the Sun that swept the valleys, in the Winds'
    encircling flight,
Recognizing holy allies, guardians of the Truth and
    Right;
While, before his face, resplendent with a firm faith's
    candid ray,
Dazzled troops of foes attendant, bow'd before him
    on his way.

But the calm physician, viewing where the white
    neck join'd the ear,

Said, " It is a slinger's doing : Sun nor Wind was
　　actor here.

Yet till God vouchsafe more certain knowledge of
　　his sovereign will,

Better deem the mystic curtain hides their wonted
　　demons still.

" Better so, perchance, than living in a clearer light,
　　like me,

But believing where perceiving, bound in what I
　　hear and see ;

Force and change in constant sequence, changing
　　atoms, changeless laws ;

Only in submissive patience waiting access to the
　　Cause.

" And, they say, Centurion Altus, when he to
　　Emania came,

And to Rome's subjection call'd us, urging Cæsar's
　　tribute claim,

Told that half the world barbarian thrills already
　　with the faith

Taught them by the godlike Syrian Cæsar lately
　　put to death.

" And the Sun, through starry stages measuring
  from the Ram and Bull,
Tells us of renewing Ages, and that Nature's time is
  full:
So, perchance, these silly breezes even now may
  swell the sail,
Brings the leavening word of Jesus westward also
  to the Gael."

THE BURIAL OF KING CORMAC.

INTRODUCTORY NOTE.

ORMAC, son of Art, son of Con Cead-Catha,* enjoyed the sovereignty of Ireland through the prolonged period of forty years, commencing from A.D. 213. During the latter part of his reign, he resided at Sletty on the Boyne, being, it is said, disqualified for the occupation of Tara by the personal blemish he had sustained in the loss of an eye, by the hand of Angus " Dread-Spear," chief of the Desi, a tribe whose original seats were in the barony of Deece, in the county of Meath. It was in the time of Cormac and his son Carbre, if we are to credit the Irish annals, that Fin, son of Comhal, and the Fenian heroes, celebrated by Ossian, flourished. Cormac has obtained the reputation of wisdom and learning, and appears justly entitled to the honour of having provoked the enmity of the Pagan priesthood, by declaring his faith in a God not made by hands of men.

---

* *i. e.* Hundred-Battle.

THE BURIAL OF KING CORMAC.

"FROM Cruach and his sub-gods twelve,"
    Said Cormac, " are but carven treene;
    The axe that made them, haft or helve,
Had worthier of our worship been.

" But He who made the tree to grow,
    And hid in earth the iron-stone,
And made the man with mind to know
    The axe's use, is God alone."

Anon to priests of Crom was brought—
    Where, girded in their service dread,
They minister'd on red Moy Slaught—
    Word of the words King Cormac said.

They loosed their curse against the king;
    They cursed him in his flesh and bones;
And daily in their mystic ring
    They turn'd the maledictive stones,[20]

Till, where at meat the monarch sate,
   Amid the revel and the wine,
He choked upon the food he ate,
   At Sletty, southward of the Boyne.

High vaunted then the priestly throng,
   And far and wide they noised abroad
With trump and loud liturgic song
   The praise of their avenging God.

But ere the voice was wholly spent
   That priest and prince should still obey,
To awed attendants o'er him bent
   Great Cormac gather'd breath to say,—

" Spread not the beds of Brugh for me [21]
   When restless death-bed's use is done :
But bury me at Rossnaree
   And face me to the rising sun.

" For all the kings who lie in Brugh
   Put trust in gods of wood and stone ;
And 'twas at Ross that first I knew
   One, Unseen, who is God alone.

" His glory lightens from the east ;
  His message soon shall reach our shore ;
And idol-god, and cursing priest
  Shall plague us from Moy Slaught no more."

Dead Cormac on his bier they laid :—
  " He reign'd a king for forty years,
And shame it were," his captains said,
  " He lay not with his royal peers.

" His grandsire, Hundred-Battle, sleeps
  Serene in Brugh : and, all around,
Dead kings in stone sepulchral keeps
  Protect the sacred burial ground.

" What though a dying man should rave
  Of changes o'er the eastern sea ?
In Brugh of Boyne shall be his grave,
  And not in noteless Rossnaree."

Then northward forth they bore the bier,
  And down from Sletty side they drew,
With horseman and with charioteer,
  To cross the fords of Boyne to Brugh.

There came a breath of finer air
　　That touch'd the Boyne with ruffling wings,
It stirr'd him in his sedgy lair
　　And in his mossy moorland springs.

And as the burial train came down
　　With dirge and savage dolorous shows,
Across their pathway, broad and brown
　　The deep, full-hearted river rose ;

From bank to bank through all his fords,
　　'Neath blackening squalls he swell'd and boil'd ;
And thrice the wondering gentile lords
　　Essay'd to cross, and thrice recoil'd.

Then forth stepp'd grey-hair'd warriors four :
　　They said, " Through angrier floods than these,
On link'd shields once our king we bore
　　From Dread-Spear and the hosts of Deece.

" And long as loyal will holds good,
　　And limbs respond with helpful thews,
Nor flood, nor fiend within the flood,
　　Shall bar him of his burial dues."

With slanted necks they stoop'd to lift;
   They heaved him up to neck and chin;
And, pair and pair, with footsteps swift,
   Lock'd arm and shoulder, bore him in.

'Twas brave to see them leave the shore;
   To mark the deep'ning surges rise,
And fall subdued in foam before
   The tension of their striding thighs.

'Twas brave, when now a spear-cast out,
   Breast-high the battling surges ran;
For weight was great, and limbs were stout,
   And loyal man put trust in man.

But ere they reach'd the middle deep,
   Nor steadying weight of clay they bore,
Nor strain of sinewy limbs could keep
   Their feet beneath the swerving four.

And now they slide, and now they swim,
   And now, amid the blackening squall,
Grey locks afloat, with clutchings grim,
   They plunge around the floating pall.

While, as a youth with practised spear
    Through justling crowds bears off the ring,
Boyne from their shoulders caught the bier
    And proudly bore away the king.

At morning, on the grassy marge
    Of Rossnaree, the corpse was found,
And shepherds at their early charge
    Entomb'd it in the peaceful ground.

A tranquil spot: a hopeful sound
    Comes from the ever youthful stream,
And still on daisied mead and mound
    The dawn delays with tenderer beam.

Round Cormac Spring renews her buds:
    In march perpetual by his side,
Down come the earth-fresh April floods,
    And up the sea-fresh salmon glide;

And life and time rejoicing run
    From age to age their wonted way;
But still he waits the risen Sun,
    For still 'tis only dawning Day.

AIDEEN'S GRAVE.

INTRODUCTORY NOTE.

AIDEEN, daughter of Angus of Ben-Edar (now the Hill of Howth), died of grief for the loss of her husband, Oscar, son of Ossian, who was slain at the battle of Gavra (*Gowra*, near Tara in Meath), A.D. 284. Oscar was entombed in the rath or earthen fortress that occupied part of the field of battle, the rest of the slain being cast in a pit outside. Aideen is said to have been buried on Howth, near the mansion of her father, and poetical tradition represents the Fenian heroes as present at her obsequies. The Cromlech in Howth Park has been supposed to be her sepulchre. It stands under the summits from which the poet Atharne is said to have launched his invectives against the people of Leinster, until, by the blighting effect of his satires, they were compelled to make him atonement for the death of his son.

AIDEEN'S GRAVE.

THEY heaved the stone; they heap'd the
cairn:
Said Ossian, " In a queenly grave
We leave her, 'mong her fields of fern,
   Between the cliff and wave.

" The cliff behind stands clear and bare,
   And bare, above, the heathery steep
Scales the clear heaven's expanse, to where
   The Danaan Druids sleep.[22]

" And all the sands that, left and right,
   The grassy isthmus-ridge confine,
In yellow bars lie bare and bright
   Among the sparkling brine.

" A clear pure air pervades the scene,
   In loneliness and awe secure;
Meet spot to sepulchre a Queen
   Who in her life was pure.

" Here, far from camp and chase removed,
  Apart in Nature's quiet room,
The music that alive she loved
  Shall cheer her in the tomb.

" The humming of the noontide bees,
  The lark's loud carol all day long,
And, borne on evening's salted breeze,
  The clanking sea bird's song

" Shall round her airy chamber float,
  And with the whispering winds and streams
Attune to Nature's tenderest note
  The tenor of her dreams.

" And oft, at tranquil eve's decline
  When full tides lip the Old Green Plain,[23]
The lowing of Moynalty's kine
  Shall round her breathe again,

" In sweet remembrance of the days
  When, duteous, in the lowly vale,
Unconscious of my Oscar's gaze,
  She fill'd the fragrant pail,

" And, duteous, from the running brook
    Drew water for the bath; nor deem'd
A king did on her labour look,
    And she a fairy seem'd.[24]

" But when the wintry frosts begin,
    And in their long drawn, lofty flight,
The wild geese with their airy din
    Distend the ear of night,

" And when the fierce De Danaan ghosts
    At midnight from their peak come down,
When all around the enchanted coasts
    Despairing strangers drown;

" When, mingling with the wreckful wail,
    From low Clontarf's wave-trampled floor
Comes booming up the burthen'd gale
    The angry Sand-Bull's roar;[25]

" Or, angrier than the sea, the shout
    Of Erin's hosts in wrath combined,
When Terror heads Oppression's rout,
    And Freedom cheers behind:—

" Then o'er our lady's placid dream,
　　Where safe from storms she sleeps, may steal
Such joy as will not misbeseem
　　A Queen of men to feel:

" Such thrill of free, defiant pride,
　　As rapt her in her battle car
At Gavra, when by Oscar's side
　　She rode the ridge of war,

" Exulting, down the shouting troops,
　　And through the thick confronting kings,
With hands on all their javelin loops
　　And shafts on all their strings;

" E'er closed the inseparable crowds,
　　No more to part for me, and show,
As bursts the sun through scattering clouds,
　　My Oscar issuing so.

" No more, dispelling battle's gloom
　　Shall son for me from fight return;
The great green rath's ten-acred tomb
　　Lies heavy on his urn.[26]

" A cup of bodkin-pencill'd clay
   Holds Oscar; mighty heart and limb
One handful now of ashes grey:
   And she has died for him.

" And here, hard by her natal bower
   On lone Ben Edar's side, we strive
With lifted rock and sign of power
   To keep her name alive.

" That while, from circling year to year,
   Her Ogham-letter'd stone is seen,
The Gael shall say, ' Our Fenians here
   Entomb'd their loved Aideen.'

" The Ogham from her pillar stone
   In tract of time will wear away;
Her name at last be only known
   In Ossian's echo'd lay.

" The long forgotten lay I sing
   May only ages hence revive,
(As eagle with a wounded wing
   To soar again might strive,)

F

" Imperfect, in an alien speech,
　　When, wandering here, some child of chance
Through pangs of keen delight shall reach
　　The gift of utterance,—

" To speak the air, the sky to speak,
　　The freshness of the hill to tell,
Who, roaming bare Ben Edar's peak
　　And Aideen's briary dell,

" And gazing on the Cromlech vast,
　　And on the mountain and the sea,
Shall catch communion with the past
　　And mix himself with me.

" Child of the Future's doubtful night,
　　Whate'er your speech, whoe'er your sires,
Sing while you may with frank delight
　　The song your hour inspires.

" Sing while you may, nor grieve to know
　　The song you sing shall also die;
Atharna's lay has perish'd so,
　　Though once it thrill'd this sky

" Above us, from his rocky chair,
　　There, where Ben Edar's landward crest
O'er eastern Bregia bends, to where
　　Dun Almon crowns the west:

" And all that felt the fretted air
　　Throughout the song-distemper'd clime,
Did droop, till suppliant Leinster's prayer
　　Appeased the vengeful rhyme.[27]

" Ah me, or e'er the hour arrive
　　Shall bid my long-forgotten tones,
Unknown One, on your lips revive,
　　Here, by these moss-grown stones,

" What change shall o'er the scene have cross'd ;
　　What conquering lords anew have come ;
What lore-arm'd, mightier Druid host
　　From Gaul or distant Rome !

" What arts of death, what ways of life,
　　What creeds unknown to bard or seer,
Shall round your careless steps be rife,
　　Who pause and ponder here ;

" And, haply, where yon curlew calls
    Athwart the marsh, 'mid groves and bowers
See rise some mighty chieftain's halls
    With unimagined towers:

" And baying hounds, and coursers bright,
    And burnish'd cars of dazzling sheen,
With courtly train of dame and knight,
    Where now the fern is green.

" Or, by yon prostrate altar-stone
    May kneel, perchance, and, free from blame,
Hear holy men with rites unknown
    New names of God proclaim.

" Let change as may the Name of Awe,
    Let rite surcease and altar fall,
The same One God remains, a law
    For ever and for all.

" Let change as may the face of earth,
    Let alter all the social frame,
For mortal men the ways of birth
    And death are still the same.

" And still, as life and time wear on,
  The children of the waning days,
(Though strength be from their shoulders gone
  To lift the loads we raise,)

" Shall weep to do the burial rites
  Of lost ones loved; and fondly found,
In shadow of the gathering nights,
  The monumental mound.

" Farewell! the strength of men is worn;
  The night approaches dark and chill:
Sleep, till perchance an endless morn
  Descend the glittering hill."

Of Oscar and Aideen bereft,
  So Ossian sang. The Fenians sped
Three mighty shouts to heaven; and left
  Ben Edar to the dead.

THE WELSHMEN OF TIRAWLEY.

INTRODUCTORY NOTE.

SEVERAL Welsh Families, associates in the invasion of Strongbow, settled in the west of Ireland. Of these, the principal whose names have been preserved by the Irish antiquarians were the Walshes, Joyces, Heils (*a quibus* Mac Hale), Lawlesses, Tomlyns, Lynotts, and Barretts, which last draw their pedigree from Walynes, son of Guyndally, the *Ard Maor*, or High Steward of the Lordship of Camelot, and had their chief seats in the territory of the two Bacs, in the barony of Tirawley, and county of Mayo. *Clochan-na-n'all*, i.e., "the Blind Men's Stepping-stones," are still pointed out on the Duvowen river, about four miles north of Crossmolina, in the townland of Garranard; and *Tubber-na-Scorney*, or "Scrag's Well," in the opposite townland of Carns, in the same barony. For a curious *terrier* or applot-ment of the Mac William's revenue, as acquired under the circumstances stated in the legend preserved by Mac Firbis, see Dr. O'Donovan's highly-learned and interesting " Genealogies, &c. of Hy Fiachrach," in the publications of the *Irish Archæological Society*—a great monument of antiquarian and topographical erudition.

THE WELSHMEN OF TIRAWLEY.

SCORNA BOY, the Barretts' bailiff,
      lewd and lame,
    To lift the Lynotts' taxes when he came,
Rudely drew a young maid to him ;
Then the Lynotts rose and slew him,
And in Tubber-na-Scorney threw him—
      Small your blame,
      Sons of Lynott !
Sing the vengeance of the Welshmen of Tirawley.

Then the Barretts to the Lynotts proposed a choice,
Saying, " Hear, ye murderous brood, men and boys,
For this deed to-day ye lose
Sight or manhood : say and choose

Which ye keep and which refuse;
                And rejoice
                That our mercy
Leaves you living for a warning to Tirawley."

Then the little boys of the Lynotts, weeping, said,
" Only leave us our eyesight in our head."
But the bearded Lynotts then
Made answer back again,
" Take our eyes, but leave us men,
                Alive or dead,
                Sons of Wattin ! "
Sing the vengeance of the Welshmen of Tirawley.

So the Barretts, with sewing-needles sharp and
        smooth,
Let the light out of the eyes of every youth,
And of every bearded man
Of the broken Lynott clan ;
Then their darken'd faces wan
                Turning south
                To the river—
Sing the vengeance of the Welshmen of Tirawley.

O'er the slippery stepping-stones of Clochan-na-n'all
They drove them, laughing loud at every fall,
As their wandering footsteps dark
Fail'd to reach the slippery mark,
And the swift stream swallow'd stark,

One and all,

As they stumbled—

From the vengeance of the Welshmen of Tirawley.

Of all the blinded Lynotts one alone
Walk'd erect from stepping-stone to stone:
So back again they brought you,
And a second time they wrought you
With their needles; but never got you

Once to groan,

Emon Lynott,

For the vengeance of the Welshmen of Tirawley.

But with prompt-projected footsteps sure as ever,
Emon Lynott again cross'd the river,
Though Duvowen was rising fast,
And the shaking stones o'ercast
By cold floods boiling past;

Yet you never,
Emon Lynott,
Faltered once before your foemen of Tirawley !

But, turning on Ballintubber bank, you stood,
And the Barretts thus bespoke o'er the flood—
" Oh, ye foolish sons of Wattin,
Small amends are these you've gotten,
For, while Scorna Boy lies rotten,
I am good
For vengeance ! "
Sing the vengeance of the Welshmen of Tirawley.

For 'tis neither in eye nor eyesight that a man
Bears the fortunes of himself and his clan,
But in the manly mind,
These darken'd orbs behind,
That your needles could never find
Though they ran
Through my heart-strings ! "
Sing the vengeance of the Welshmen of Tirawley.

" But, little your women's needles do I reck :
For the night from heaven never fell so black,
But Tirawley, and abroad
From the Moy to Cuan-an-fod,[28]

I could walk it, every sod,
>> Path and track,
>> Ford and togher,
Seeking vengeance on you, Barretts of Tirawley !

"The night when Dathy O'Dowda broke your camp,
What Barrett among you was it held the lamp—
Show'd the way to those two feet,
When through wintry wind and sleet,
I guided your blind retreat
>> In the swamp
>> Of Beäl-an-asa ?
O ye vengeance-destined ingrates of Tirawley !"

So leaving loud-shriek-echoing Garranard,
The Lynott like a red dog hunted hard,
With his wife and children seven,
'Mong the beasts and fowls of heaven
In the hollows of Glen Nephin,
>> Light-debarr'd,
>> Made his dwelling,
Planning vengeance on the Barretts of Tirawley.

And ere the bright-orb'd year its course had run,
On his brown round-knotted knee he nurs'd a son,

A child of light, with eyes
As clear as are the skies
In summer, when sunrise
        Has begun ;
        So the Lynott
Nursed his vengeance on the Barretts of Tirawley.

And, as ever the bright boy grew in strength and
        size,
Made him perfect in each manly exercise,
The salmon in the flood,
The dun deer in the wood,
The eagle in the cloud
        To surprise,
        On Ben Nephin,
Far above the foggy fields of Tirawley.

With the yellow-knotted spear-shaft, with the bow,
With the steel, prompt to deal shot and blow,
He taught him from year to year
And train'd him, without a peer,
For a perfect cavalier,
        Hoping so—
        Far his forethought—
For vengeance on the Barretts of Tirawley.

And, when mounted on his proud-bounding steed,
Emon Oge sat a cavalier indeed;
Like the ear upon the wheat
When winds in Autumn beat
On the bending stems, his seat;
    And the speed
     Of his courser
Was the wind from Barna-na-gee [29] o'er Tirawley!

Now when fifteen sunny summers thus were spent,
(He perfected in all accomplishment)—
The Lynott said, " My child,
We are over long exiled
From mankind in this wild—
    —Time we went
     Through the mountain
To the countries lying over-against Tirawley."

So, out over mountain-moors, and mosses brown,
And green stream-gathering vales, they journey'd
    down;
Till, shining like a star,
Through the dusky gleams afar,

The bailey of Castlebar,
>>And the town
>>Of Mac William
Rose bright before the wanderers of Tirawley.

" Look southward, my boy, and tell me as we go,
What seest thou by the loch-head below."
" Oh, a stone-house strong and great,
And a horse-host at the gate,
And their captain in armour of plate—
>>Grand the show !
>>Great the glancing !
High the heroes of this land below Tirawley !

" And a beautiful Woman-chief by his side,
Yellow gold on all her gown-sleeves wide ;
And in her hand a pearl
Of a young, little, fair-hair'd girl."—
Said the Lynott, " It is the Earl !
>>Let us ride
>>To his presence !"
And before him came the exiles of Tirawley.

" God save thee, Mac William," the Lynott thus
>>began ;
" God save all here besides of this clan ;

For gossips dear to me
Are all in company—
For in these four bones ye see
> A kindly man
> Of the Britons—
Emon Lynott of Garranard of Tirawley.

" And hither, as kindly gossip-law allows,
I come to claim a scion of thy house
To foster; for thy race,
Since William Conquer's[30] days,
Have ever been wont to place,
> With some spouse
> Of a Briton,
A Mac William Oge, to foster in Tirawley.

" And to show thee in what sort our youth are
> taught,
I have hither to thy home of valour brought
This one son of my age,
For a sample and a pledge
For the equal tutelage,
> In right thought,
> Word, and action,
Of whatever son ye give into Tirawley."

When Mac William beheld the brave boy ride and
       run,
Saw the spear-shaft from his white shoulder spun—
With a sigh, and with a smile,
He said,—" I would give the spoil
Of a county, that Tibbot* Moyle,
              My own son,
              Were accomplish'd
Like this branch of the kindly Britons of Tirawley."

When the Lady Mac William she heard him speak,
And saw the ruddy roses on his cheek,
She said, " I would give a purse
Of red gold to the nurse
That would rear my Tibbot no worse;
              But I seek
              Hitherto vainly—
Heaven grant that I now have found her in
       Tirawley ! "

So they said to the Lynott, " Here, take our bird !
And as pledge for the keeping of thy word,
Let this scion here remain
Till thou comest back again:

---

* Tibbot, that is, Theobald.

Meanwhile the fitting train
   Of a lord
   Shall attend thee
With the lordly heir of Connaught into Tirawley."

So back to strong-throng-gathering Garranard,
Like a lord of the country with his guard,
Came the Lynott, before them all.
Once again over Clochan-na-n'all,
Steady-striding, erect, and tall,
   And his ward
   On his shoulders;
To the wonder of the Welshmen of Tirawley.

Then a diligent foster-father you would deem
The Lynott, teaching Tibbot, by mead and stream,
To cast the spear, to ride,
To stem the rushing tide,
With what feats of body beside,
   Might beseem
   A Mac William,
Foster'd free among the Welshmen of Tirawley.

But the lesson of hell he taught him in heart and
        mind;
For to what desire soever he inclined,
Of anger, lust, or pride,
He had it gratified,
Till he ranged the circle wide
            Of a blind
            Self-indulgence,
Ere he came to youthful manhood in Tirawley.

Then, even as when a hunter slips a hound,
Lynott loosed him—God's leashes all unbound—
In the pride of power and station,
And the strength of youthful passion,
On the daughters of thy nation,
            All around,
            Wattin Barrett!
Oh! the vengeance of the Welshmen of Tirawley!

Bitter grief and burning anger, rage and shame,
Fill'd the houses of the Barretts where'er he came;
Till the young men of the Bac
Drew by night upon his track,

And slew him at Cornassack—[31]
   Small your blame,
   Sons of Wattin !
Sing the vengeance of the Welshmen of Tirawley.

Said the Lynott, " The day of my vengeance is
   drawing near,
The day for which, through many a long dark year,
I have toil'd through grief and sin—
Call ye now the Brehons in,
And let the plea begin
   Over the bier
   Of Mac William,
For an eric upon the Barretts of Tirawley.[32]

Then the Brehons to Mac William Burk decreed
An eric upon Clan Barrett for the deed;
And the Lynott's share of the fine,
As foster-father, was nine
Ploughlands and nine score kine;
   But no need
   Had the Lynott,
Neither care, for land or cattle in Tirawley.

But rising, while all sat silent on the spot,
He said, " The law says—doth it not?—
If the foster-sire elect
His portion to reject,
He may then the right exact
      To applot
      The short eric."
" 'Tis the law," replied the Brehons of Tirawley.

Said the Lynott, " I once before had a choice
Proposed me, wherein law had little voice;
But now I choose, and say,
As lawfully I may,
I applot the mulct to-day;
      So rejoice
      In your ploughlands
And your cattle which I renounce throughout
      Tirawley.

" And thus I applot the mulct: I divide
The land throughout Clan Barrett on every side
Equally, that no place
May be without the face

Of a foe of Wattin's race—
        That the pride
        Of the Barretts
May be humbled hence for ever throughout
      Tirawley.

" I adjudge a seat in every Barrett's hall
To Mac William: in every stable I give a stall
To Mac William: and, beside,
Whenever a Burke shall ride
Through Tirawley, I provide
        At his call
        Needful grooming,
Without charge from any hosteler of Tirawley.

" Thus lawfully I avenge me for the throes
Ye lawlessly caused me and caused those
Unhappy shamefaced ones,
Who, their mothers expected once,
Would have been the sires of sons—
        O'er whose woes
        Often weeping,
I have groan'd in my exile from Tirawley.

" I demand not of you your manhood; but I
        take—
For the Burkes will take it—your Freedom! for the
        sake
Of which all manhood's given,
And all good under heaven,
And, without which, better even
                Ye should make
                Yourselves barren,
Than see your children slaves throughout Tirawley!

" Neither take I your eyesight from you; as you
        took
Mine and ours: I would have you daily look
On one another's eyes,
When the strangers tyrannize
By your hearths, and blushes arise,
                That ye brook,
                Without vengeance,
The insults of troops of Tibbots throughout
        Tirawley!

" The vengeance I design'd, now is done,
And the days of me and mine nearly run—

For, for this, I have broken faith,
Teaching him who lies beneath
This pall, to merit death;
   And my son
   To his father
Stands pledged for other teaching in Tirawley."

Said Mac William—" Father and son, hang them
  high !"
And the Lynott they hang'd speedily;
But across the salt sea water,
To Scotland, with the daughter
Of Mac William—well you got her !—
   Did you fly,
   Edmund Lindsay,
The gentlest of all the Welshmen of Tirawley !

'Tis thus the ancient Ollaves of Erin tell [33]
How, through lewdness and revenge, it befell
That the sons of William Conquer
Came over the sons of Wattin,
Throughout all the bounds and borders
Of the land of Auley Mac Fiachra; *
Till the Saxon Oliver Cromwell,

   * *Pronounced* Mac Eĕăra.

And his valiant, Bible-guided,
Free heretics of Clan London
Coming in, in their succession,
Rooted out both Burke and Barrett,
And in their empty places
New stems of freedom planted,
With many a goodly sapling
Of manliness and virtue;
Which while their children cherish,
Kindly Irish of the Irish,
Neither Saxons nor Italians,
May the mighty God of Freedom
            Speed them well,
            Never taking
Further vengeance on his people of Tirawley.

OWEN BAWN.

INTRODUCTORY NOTE.

WILLIAM DE BURGHO, third Earl of Ulster, pursued the Anglican policy of his day with so much severity, that the native Irish generally withdrew from the counties of Down and Antrim, and established themselves in Tyrone with Hugh Boy O'Neill. William's rigid prohibition of intermarriages with the natives led to his assassination by his own relatives, the Mandevilles, at the Ford of Belfast, A.D. 1333. The Irish then returned from beyond the river Bann, and expelled the English from all Ulster, except Carrickfergus and the barony of Ards in Down; and so continued until their subjugation by Sir Henry Sidney and Sir Arthur Chichester, in the reign of Queen Elizabeth.

Simultaneously with the return of the Clan Hugh-Boy in the north, the great Anglo-Norman families of Connaught adopted Irish names and manners, the De Burghos assuming the name of Mac William, and all accommodating

themselves to the Irish system of life and government, in
which, with few exceptions, they continued until *their*
subjugation by Sir Richard Bingham, in the reign of
King Henry the Eighth.

OWEN BAWN.

MY Owen Bawn's hair is of thread of gold
          spun ;
    Of gold in the shadow, of light in the
      sun ;
All curl'd in a coolun the bright tresses are—
They make his head radiant with beams like a
      star !

My Owen Bawn's mantle is long and is wide,
To wrap me up safe from the storm by his side ;
And I'd rather face snow-drift and winter-wind
          there,
Than lie among daisies and sunshine elsewhere.

My Owen Bawn Quin is a hunter of deer,
He tracts the dun quarry with arrow and spear—

Where wild woods are waving, and deep waters
    flow,
Ah, there goes my love with the dun-dappled roe.

My Owen Bawn Quin is a bold fisherman,
He spears the strong salmon in midst of the Bann;
And rock'd in the tempest on stormy Lough Neagh,
Draws up the red trout through the bursting of
    spray.

My Owen Bawn Quin is a bard of the best,
He wakes me with singing, he sings me to rest;
And the cruit 'neath his fingers rings up with a
    sound,
As though angels harp'd o'er us, and fays under-
    ground.

They tell me the stranger has given command,
That crommeal and coolun shall cease in the land,
That all our youths' tresses of yellow be shorn,
And bonnets, instead, of a new fashion, worn;

That mantles like Owen Bawn's shield us no more,
That hunting and fishing henceforth we give o'er,

That the net and the arrow aside must be laid,
For hammer and trowel, and mattock and spade;

That the echoes of music must sleep in their caves,
That the slave must forget his own tongue for a
    slave's,
That the sounds of our lips must be strange in our
    ears,
And our bleeding hands toil in the dew of our tears.

Oh sweetheart and comfort! with thee by my side,
I could love and live happy, whatever betide;
But *thou*, in such bondage, wouldst die ere a day—
Away to Tir-oën, then, Owen, away!

There are wild woods and mountains, and streams
    deep and clear,
There are loughs in Tir-oën as lovely as here;
There are silver harps ringing in Yellow Hugh's
    hall,
And a bower by the forest side, sweetest of all!

We will dwell by the sunshiny skirts of the brake,
Where the sycamore shadows glow deep in the lake;

And the snowy swan stirring the green shadows
there,
Afloat on the water, seems floating in air.

Away to Tir-oën, then, Owen, away!
We will leave them the dust from our feet for a
prey,
And our dwelling in ashes and flames for a spoil—
'Twill be long ere they quench them with streams
of the Foyle!

GRACE O'MALY.

INTRODUCTORY NOTE.

THE return to English rule and habits of the Anglo-Norman families of Connaught who had Hibernicised after the murder of William de Burgho, was not effected without a long alienation of the popular affections which had been bestowed upon them as freely as on native rulers: " for," to use the words of a contemporary Irish chronicler, " the old chieftains of Erin prospered under these princely English lords who were our chief rulers, and who had given up their foreignness for a pure mind, and their surliness for good manners, and their stubbornness for sweet mildness, and who had given up their perverseness for hospitality."* During this troubled period of transition, Grace O'Maly, lady of Sir Rickard Burke, styled Mac William *Eighter*, distinguished herself by a life of wayward adventure which has made her name, in its Gaelic form, *Grana Uaile* (i. e. *Grana Ua Mhaile*,) a personifica-

---

* O'Donovan, *Tr. and Cust.* of *Hy Many*, p. 136.

tion, among the Irish peasantry, of that social state which
they still consider preferable to the results of a more
advanced civilization. The real acts and character of
the heroine are hardly seen through the veil of imagina-
tion under which the personified idea exists in the popu-
lar mind, and is here presented.

GRACE O'MALY.

SHE left the close-air'd land of trees
　　And proud Mac William's palace,
　For clear, bare Clare's health-salted breeze,
　Her oarsmen and her galleys:
And where, beside the bending strand
　　The rock and billow wrestle,
Between the deep sea and the land
　　She built her Island Castle.

The Spanish captains, sailing by
　　For Newport, with amazement
Beheld the cannon'd longship lie
　　Moor'd to the lady's casement;
And, covering coin and cup of gold
　　In haste their hatches under,

They whisper'd " Tis a pirate's hold;
 She sails the seas for plunder!"

But no: 'twas not for sordid spoil
 Of barque or sea-board borough
She plough'd, with unfatiguing toil,
 The fluent-rolling furrow;
Delighting, on the broad-back'd deep,
 To feel the quivering galley
Strain up the opposing hill, and sweep
 Down the withdrawing valley:

Or, sped before a driving blast,
 By following seas uplifted,
Catch, from the huge heaps heaving past,
 And from the spray they drifted,
And from the winds that toss'd the crest
 Of each wide-shouldering giant,
The smack of freedom and the zest
 Of rapturous life defiant.

For, oh! the mainland time was pent
 In close constraint and striving:—
So many aims together bent
 On winning and on thriving;

There was no room for generous ease,
    No sympathy for candour;—
And so she left Burke's buzzing trees,
    And all his stony splendour.

For Erin yet had fields to spare,
    Where Clew her cincture gathers
Isle-gemm'd; and kindly clans were there
    The fosterers of her fathers:
Room there for careless feet to roam
    Secure from minions' peeping,
For fearless mirth to find a home
    And sympathetic weeping;

And generous ire and frank disdain
    To speak the mind, nor ponder
How this in England, that in Spain,
    Might suit to tell; as yonder,
Where daily on the slippery dais
    By thwarting interests chequer'd,
State gamesters play the social chess
    Of politic Clanrickard.

Nor wanting quite the lonely isle
    In civic life's adornings:

H

The Brehon's Court might well beguile
 A learned lady's mornings.
Quaint though the clamorous claim, and rude
 The pleading that convey'd it,
Right conscience made the judgment good,
 And loyal love obey'd it.

And music sure was sweeter far
 For ears of native nurture,
Than virginals at Castlebar
 To tinkling touch of courtier,
When harpers good in hall struck up
 The planxty's gay commotion,
Or pipers scream'd from pennon'd poop
 Their piobroch over ocean.

And sweet to see, their ruddy bloom
 Whom ocean's friendly distance
Preserved still unenslaved; for whom
 No tasking of existence
Made this one rich, and that one poor,
 In gold's illusive treasure,
But all, of easy life secure,
 Were rich in wealth of leisure.

Rich in the Muse's pensive hour,
  In genial hour for neighbour,
Rich in young mankind's happy power
  To live with little labour;
The wise, free way of life, indeed,
  That still, with charm adaptive,
Reclaims and tames the alien greed,
  And takes the conqueror captive.

Nor only life's unclouded looks
  To compensate its rudeness;
Amends there were in holy books,
  In offices of goodness,
In cares above the transient scene
  Of little gains and honours,
That well repaid the Island Queen
  Her loss of urban manners.

Sweet, when the crimson sunsets glow'd,
  As earth and sky grew grander,
Adown the grass'd, unechoing road
  Atlanticward to wander,
Some kinsman's humbler hearth to seek,
  Some sick-bed side, it may be,
Or, onward reach, with footsteps meek,
  The low, grey, lonely abbey:

And, where the storied stone beneath
   The guise of plant and creature,
Had fused the harder lines of faith
   In easy forms of nature;
Such forms as tell the master's pains
   'Mong Roslin's carven glories,
Or hint the faith of Pictish Thanes
   On standing stones of Forres;

The Branch; the weird cherubic Beasts;
   The Hart by hounds o'ertaken;
Or, intimating mystic feasts,
   The self-resorbent Dragon;—
Mute symbols, though with power endow'd
   For finer dogmas' teaching,
Than clerk might tell to carnal crowd
   In homily or preaching;—

Sit; and while heaven's refulgent show
   Grew airier and more tender,
And ocean's gleaming floor below
   Reflected loftier splendour,
Suffused with light of lingering faith
   And ritual light's reflection,
Discourse of birth, and life, and death,
   And of the resurrection.

But chiefly sweet from morn to eve,
From eve to clear-eyed morning,
The presence of the felt reprieve
From strangers' note and scorning:
No prying, proud, intrusive foes
To pity and offend her:—
Such was the life the lady chose;
Such choosing, we commend her.

BALLADS AND POEMS.

THE FAIRY THORN.

AN ULSTER BALLAD.

"GET up, our Anna dear, from the weary
    spinning-wheel;
  For your father's on the hill, and your
    mother is asleep:
Come up above the crags, and we'll dance a high-
    land reel
  Around the fairy thorn on the steep."

At Anna Grace's door 'twas thus the maidens cried,
  Three merry maidens fair in kirtles of the green;
And Anna laid the rock and the weary wheel aside,
  The fairest of the four, I ween.

They're glancing through the glimmer of the quiet
    eve,
  Away in milky wavings of neck and ancle bare;

The heavy-sliding stream in its sleepy song they
    leave,
  And the crags in the ghostly air :

And linking hand and hand, and singing as they go,
  The maids along the hill-side have ta'en their
      fearless way,
Till they come to where the rowan trees in lonely
    beauty grow
  Beside the Fairy Hawthorn grey.

The Hawthorn stands between the ashes tall and
    slim,
  Like matron with her twin grand-daughters at
      her knee;
The rowan berries cluster o'er her low head grey
    and dim
  In ruddy kisses sweet to see.

The merry maidens four have ranged them in a row,
  Between each lovely couple a stately rowan stem,
And away in mazes wavy, like skimming birds
    they go,
  Oh, never caroll'd bird like them !

But solemn is the silence of the silvery haze
    That drinks away their voices in echoless repose,
And dreamily the evening has still'd the haunted
        braes,
    And dreamier the gloaming grows.

And sinking one by one, like lark-notes from the
        sky
    When the falcon's shadow saileth across the open
        shaw,
Are hush'd the maiden's voices, as cowering down
        they lie
    In the flutter of their sudden awe.

For, from the air above, and the grassy ground be-
        neath,
    And from the mountain-ashes and the old White-
        thorn between,
A Power of faint enchantment doth through their
        beings breathe,
    And they sink down together on the green.

They sink together silent, and stealing side to side,
    They fling their lovely arms o'er their drooping
        necks so fair,

Then vainly strive again their naked arms to hide,
　For their shrinking necks again are bare.

Thus clasp'd and prostrate all, with their heads to-
　　　gether bow'd,
　Soft o'er their bosom's beating—the only human
　　sound—
They hear the silky footsteps of the silent fairy
　　crowd,
　Like a river in the air, gliding round.

No scream can any raise, nor prayer can any say,
　But wild, wild, the terror of the speechless three—
For they feel fair Anna Grace drawn silently away,
　By whom they dare not look to see.

They feel their tresses twine with her parting locks
　　　of gold,
　And the curls elastic falling, as her head with-
　　draws;
They feel her sliding arms from their tranced arms
　　unfold,
　But they may not look to see the cause:

For heavy on their senses the faint enchantment
  lies
    Through all that night of anguish and perilous
      amaze;
And neither fear nor wonder can ope their quivering
  eyes
    Or their limbs from the cold ground raise,

Till out of night the earth has roll'd her dewy side,
    With every haunted mountain and streamy vale
      below;
When, as the mist dissolves in the yellow morning
  tide,
    The maidens' trance dissolveth so.

Then fly the ghastly three as swiftly as they may,
    And tell their tale of sorrow to anxious friends in
      vain—
They pined away and died within the year and day,
    And ne'er was Anna Grace seen again.

WILLY GILLILAND.

AN ULSTER BALLAD.

UP in the mountain solitudes, and in a
      rebel ring,
    He has worshipp'd God upon the hill,
  in spite of church and king;
And seal'd his treason with his blood on Bothwell
    bridge he hath;
So he must fly his father's land, or he must die the
    death;
For comely Claverhouse has come along with grim
    Dalzell,
And his smoking rooftree testifies they've done their
    errand well.

In vain to fly his enemies he fled his native land;
Hot persecution waited him upon the Carrick strand;

His name was on the Carrick cross, a price was on
 his head,
A fortune to the man that brings him in alive or
 dead !
And so on moor and mountain, from the Lagan to
 the Bann,
From house to house, and hill to hill, he lurk'd an
 outlaw'd man.

At last, when in false company he might no longer
 bide,
He stay'd his houseless wanderings upon the Collon
 side,
There in a cave all underground he lair'd his heathy
 den,
Ah, many a gentleman was fain to earth like hill
 fox then !
With hound and fishing-rod he lived on hill and
 stream by day ;
At night, betwixt his fleet greyhound and his bonny
 mare he lay.

It was a summer evening, and, mellowing and still,
Glenwhirry to the setting sun lay bare from hill to
 hill ;

For all that valley pastoral held neither house nor
    tree,
But spread abroad and open all, a full fair sight to
    see,
From Slemish foot to Collon top lay one unbroken
    green,
Save where in many a silver coil the river glanced
    between.

And on the river's grassy bank, even from the
    morning grey,
He at the angler's pleasant sport had spent the
    summer day :
Ah ! many a time and oft I've spent the summer
    day from dawn,
And wonder'd, when the sunset came, where time
    and care had gone,
Along the reaches curling fresh, the wimpling pools
    and streams,
Where he that day his cares forgot in those delight-
    ful dreams.

His blithe work done, upon a bank the outlaw
    rested now,

And laid the basket from his back, the bonnet from
      his brow;
And there, his hand upon the Book, his knee upon
      the sod,
He fill'd the lonely valley with the gladsome word
      of God;
And for a persecuted kirk, and for her martyrs
      dear,
And against a godless church and king he spoke up
      loud and clear.

And now, upon his homeward way, he cross'd the
      Collon high,
And over bush and bank and brae he sent abroad
      his eye;
But all was darkening peacefully in grey and purple
      haze,
The thrush was silent in the banks, the lark upon
      the braes—
When suddenly shot up a blaze, from the cave's
      mouth it came;
And troopers' steeds and troopers' caps are glancing
      in the same!

He couch'd among the heather, and he saw them,
    as he lay,
With three long yells at parting, ride lightly east
    away:
Then down with heavy heart he came, to sorry
    cheer came he,
For ashes black were crackling where the green
    whins used to be,
And stretch'd among the prickly coomb, his heart's
    blood smoking round,
From slender nose to breast-bone cleft, lay dead his
    good greyhound!

" They've slain my dog, the Philistines! they've
    ta'en my bonny mare!"—
He plung'd into the smoky hole; no bonny beast
    was there—
He groped beneath his burning bed, (it burn'd him
    to the bone,)
Where his good weapon used to be, but broadsword
    there was none;
He reel'd out of the stifling den, and sat down on a
    stone,
And in the shadows of the night 'twas thus he made
    his moan—

" I am a houseless outcast; I have neither bed nor
        board,
Nor living thing to look upon, nor comfort save the
        Lord :
Yet many a time were better men in worse extremity ;
Who succour'd them in their distress, He now will
        succour me,—
He now will succour me, I know ; and, by His
        holy Name,
I'll make the doers of this deed right dearly rue the
        same !

" My bonny mare ! I've ridden you when Claver'se
        rode behind,
And from the thumbscrew and the boot you bore me
        like the wind ;
And, while I have the life you saved, on your sleek
        flank, I swear,
Episcopalian rowel shall never ruffle hair !
Though sword to wield they've left me none—yet
        Wallace wight, I wis,
Good battle did on Irvine side wi' waur weapon
        than this."—

His fishing-rod with both his hands he griped it as
      he spoke,

And, where the butt and top were spliced, in pieces
      twain he broke;

The limber top he cast away, with all its gear
      abroad,

But, grasping the tough hickory butt, with spike of
      iron shod,

He ground the sharp spear to a point; then pull'd
      his bonnet down,

And, meditating black revenge, set forth for Carrick
      town.

The sun shines bright on Carrick wall and Carrick
      Castle grey,

And up thine aisle, St. Nicholas, has ta'en his
      morning way,

And to the North-Gate sentinel displayeth far and
      near

Sea, hill, and tower, and all thereon, in dewy
      freshness clear,

Save where, behind a ruin'd wall, himself alone to
      view,

Is peering from the ivy green a bonnet of the blue.

The sun shines red on Carrick wall and Carrick
       Castle old,
And all the western buttresses have changed their
       grey for gold;
And from thy shrine, Saint Nicholas, the pilgrim
       of the sky
Has gone in rich farewell, as fits such royal votary;
But, as his last red glance he takes down past black
       Slieve-a-true,
He leaveth where he found it first, the bonnet of the
       blue.

Again he makes the turrets grey stand out before
       the hill;
Constant as their foundation rock, there is the bon-
       net still!
And now the gates are open'd, and forth in gallant
       show
Prick jeering grooms and burghers blythe, and
       troopers in a row;
But one has little care for jest, so hard bested
       is he,
To ride the outlaw's bonny mare, for this at last is
       she!

Down comes her master with a roar, her rider with
      a groan,
The iron and the hickory are through and through
      him gone !
He lies a corpse; and where he sat, the outlaw sits
      again,
And once more to his bonny mare he gives the spur
      and rein ;
Then some with sword, and some with gun, they
      ride and run amain ;
But sword and gun, and whip and spur, that day
      they plied in vain !

Ah ! little thought Willy Gilliland, when he on
      Skerry side
Drew bridle first, and wiped his brow after that
      weary ride,
That where he lay like hunted brute, a cavern'd
      outlaw lone,
Broad lands and yeoman tenantry should yet be
      there his own :
Yet so it was ; and still from him descendants not
      a few
Draw birth and lands, and, let me trust, draw love
      of Freedom too.

THE FORGING OF THE ANCHOR.

COME, see the Dolphin's anchor forged—
    'tis at a white heat now :
    The bellows ceased, the flames de-
creased—though on the forge's brow
The little flames still fitfully play through the sable
    mound,
And fitfully you still may see the grim smiths
    ranking round,
All clad in leathern panoply, their broad hands only
    bare :
Some rest upon their sledges here, some work the
    windlass there.

The windlass strains the tackle chains, the black
    mound heaves below,
And red and deep a hundred veins burst out at every
    throe :

It rises, roars, rends all outright—O, Vulcan, what
     a glow!

'Tis blinding white, 'tis blasting bright—the high
     sun shines not so!

The high sun sees not, on the earth, such fiery fear-
     ful show,

The roof-ribs swarth, the candent hearth, the ruddy
     lurid row

Of smiths that stand, an ardent band, like men be-
     fore the foe,

As, quivering through his fleece of flame, the
     sailing monster, slow

Sinks on the anvil:—all about the faces fiery grow;

" Hurrah!" they shout, " leap out—leap out;"
     bang, bang the sledges go:

Hurrah! the jetted lightnings are hissing high and
     low—

A hailing fount of fire is struck at every squashing
     blow;

The leathern mail rebounds the hail, the rattling
     cinders strow

The ground around; at every bound the sweltering
     fountains flow,

And thick and loud the swinking crowd at every
     stroke pant " ho!"

Leap out, leap out, my masters; leap out and lay
    on load!

Let's forge a goodly anchor—a bower thick and
    broad;

For a heart of oak is hanging on every blow, I bode:

I see the good ship riding all in a perilous
    road—

The low reef roaring on her lee—the roll of ocean
    pour'd

From stem to stern, sea after sea, the mainmast by
    the board,

The bulwarks down, the rudder gone, the boats
    stove at the chains!

But courage still, brave mariners—the bower yet
    remains,

And not an inch to flinch he deigns, save when ye
    pitch sky high;

Then moves his head, as though he said, " Fear
    nothing—here am I."

Swing in your strokes in order, let foot and hand
    keep time;

Your blows make music sweeter far than any
    steeple's chime:

But, while you sling your sledges, sing—and let
    the burthen be,

The anchor is the anvil-king, and royal craftsmen
  we !

Strike in, strike in—the sparks begin to dull their
  rustling red ;

Our hammers ring with sharper din, our work will
  soon be sped.

Our anchor soon must change his bed of fiery rich
  array,

For a hammock at the roaring bows, or an oozy
  couch of clay ;

Our anchor soon must change the lay of merry
  craftsmen here,

For the yeo-heave-o', and the heave-away, and the
  sighing seaman's cheer ;

When, weighing slow, at eve they go—far, far from
  love and home ;

And sobbing sweethearts, in a row, wail o'er the
  ocean foam.

In livid and obdurate gloom he darkens down at
  last :

A shapely one he is, and strong, as e'er from cat was
  cast :

O trusted and trustworthy guard, if thou hadst life
    like me,
What pleasures would thy toils reward beneath the
    deep green sea !
O deep-Sea-diver, who might then behold such
    sights as thou ?
The hoary monster's palaces ! methinks what joy
    'twere now
To go plumb plunging down amid the assembly of
    the whales,
And feel the churn'd sea round me boil beneath
    their scourging tails !
Then deep in tangle-woods to fight the fierce sea
    unicorn,
And send him foil'd and bellowing back, for all his
    ivory horn :
To leave the subtle sworder-fish of bony blade
    forlorn ;
And for the ghastly-grinning shark, to laugh his
    jaws to scorn :
To leap down on the kraken's back, where 'mid
    Norwegian isles
He lies, a lubber anchorage for sudden shallow'd
    miles ;

Till snorting, like an under-sea volcano, off he
    rolls;
Meanwhile to swing, a-buffeting the far astonished
    shoals
Of his back-browsing ocean-calves; or, haply, in a
    cove,
Shell-strown, and consecrate of old to some Undiné's
    love,
To find the long-hair'd mermaidens; or, hard by
    icy lands,
To wrestle with the Sea-serpent, upon cerulean
    sands.

O broad-arm'd Fisher of the deep, whose sports can
    equal thine?
The Dolphin weighs a thousand tons, that tugs thy
    cable line;
And night by night, 'tis thy delight, thy glory day
    by day,
Through sable sea and breaker white the giant
    game to play—
But shamer of our little sports! forgive the name I
    gave—
A fisher's joy is to destroy—thine office is to save.

O lodger in the sea-kings' halls, couldst thou but
      understand

Whose be the white bones by thy side, or who that
      dripping band,

Slow swaying in the heaving wave, that round about
      thee bend,

With sounds like breakers in a dream blessing their
      ancient friend—

Oh, couldst thou know what heroes glide with
      larger steps round thee,

Thine iron side would swell with pride; thou'dst
      leap within the sea!

Give honour to their memories who left the pleasant
      strand,

To shed their blood so freely for the love of Father-
      land—

Who left their chance of quiet age and grassy
      churchyard grave,

So freely, for a restless bed amid the tossing wave—

Oh, though our anchor may not be all I have fondly
      sung,

Honour him for their memory, whose bones he
      goes among!

THE FORESTER'S COMPLAINT.

THROUGH our wild wood-walks here,
　　Sunbright and shady,
Free as the forest deer
　　Roams a lone lady:
Far from her castle-keep,
　　Down in the valley,
Roams she, by dingle deep,
　　Green holm and alley,
With her sweet presence bright
　　Gladd'ning my dwelling—
Oh, fair her face of light,
　　Past the tongue's telling!
　　　　Woe was me
　　　　E'er to see
Beauty so shining;
　　Ever since, hourly,
Have I been pining!

In our blithe sports' debates
    Down by the river,
I, of my merry mates,
    Foremost was ever;
Skilfullest with my flute,
    Leading the maidens
Heark'ning, by moonlight, mute,
    To its sweet cadence:
Sprightliest in the dance
    Tripping together—
Such a one was I once
    Ere she came hither!
      Woe was me
      E'er to see
Beauty so shining;
    Ever since, hourly,
Have I been pining!

Loud now my comrades laugh
    As I pass by them;
Broadsword and quarter-staff
    No more I ply them:
Coy now the maidens frown
    Wanting their dances;

How can their faces brown
    Win one, who fancies
Even an angel's face
    Dark to be seen would
Be, by the Lily-grace
    Gladd'ning the greenwood?
        Woe was me
        E'er to see
Beauty so shining;
    Ever since, hourly,
Have I been pining!

Wolf, by my broken bow
    Idle is lying,
While through the woods I go,
    All the day, sighing,
Tracing her footsteps small
    Through the moss'd cover,
Hiding then, breathless all,
    At the sight of her,
Lest my rude gazing should
    From her haunt scare her—
Oh, what a solitude
    Wanting her, there were!

Woe was me
E'er to see
Beauty so shining;
Ever since, hourly,
Have I been pining!

THE PRETTY GIRL OF LOCH DAN.

THE shades of eve had cross'd the glen
    That frowns o'er infant Avonmore,
    When, nigh Loch Dan, two weary men,
We stopp'd before a cottage door.

" God save all here," my comrade cries,
    And rattles on the raised latch-pin;
" God save you kindly," quick replies
    A clear sweet voice, and asks us in.

We enter; from the wheel she starts,
    A rosy girl with soft black eyes;
Her fluttering court'sy takes our hearts,
    Her blushing grace and pleased surprise.

Poor Mary, she was quite alone,
    For, all the way to Glenmalure,
Her mother had that morning gone
    And left the house in charge with her.

But neither household cares, nor yet
　The shame that startled virgins feel,
Could make the generous girl forget
　Her wonted hospitable zeal.

She brought us in a beechen bowl
　Sweet milk that smack'd of mountain thyme,
Oat cake, and such a yellow roll
　Of butter—it gilds all my rhyme !

And, while we ate the grateful food,
　(With weary limbs on bench reclined,)
Considerate and discreet, she stood
　Apart, and listen'd to the wind.

Kind wishes both our souls engaged,
　From breast to breast spontaneous ran
The mutual thought—we stood and pledged
　THE MODEST ROSE ABOVE LOCH DAN.

" The milk we drink is not more pure,
　Sweet Mary—bless those budding charms !
Than your own generous heart, I'm sure,
　Nor whiter than the breast it warms !"

She turn'd and gazed, unused to hear
  Such language in that homely glen;
But, Mary, you have nought to fear,
  Though smiled on by two stranger men.

Not for a crown would I alarm
  Your virgin pride by word or sign,
Nor need a painful blush disarm
  My friend of thoughts as pure as mine.

Her simple heart could not but feel
  The words we spoke were free from guile;
She stoop'd, she blush'd—she fix'd her wheel,
  'Tis all in vain—she can't but smile!

Just like sweet April's dawn appears
  Her modest face—I see it yet—
And though I lived a hundred years,
  Methinks I never could forget

The pleasure that, despite her heart,
  Fills all her downcast eyes with light,
The lips reluctantly apart,
  The white teeth struggling into sight,

The dimples eddying o'er her cheek,—
　　The rosy cheek that won't be still!—
Oh! who could blame what flatterers speak,
　　Did smiles like this reward their skill?

For such another smile, I vow,
　　Though loudly beats the midnight rain,
I'd take the mountain-side e'en now,
　　And walk to Luggelaw again!

HUNGARY.

AUGUST, 1849.

AWAY! would you own the dread rapture
of war,
Seek the host-rolling plain of the mighty
Magyar;
Where the giants of yore from their mansions come
down,
O'er the ocean-wide floor play the game of renown.

Hark! hark! how the earth 'neath their armament
reels,
In the hurricane charge—in the thunder of wheels;
How the hearts of the forests rebound as they pass,
In their mantle of smoke, through the quaking
morass!

God! the battle is join'd! Lord Sabaoth, rejoice!
Freedom thunders her hymn in the battery's voice—

In the soaring hurrah—in the blood-stifled moan—
Sends the voice of her praise to the foot of thy
    throne.

Oh hear, God of freedom, thy people's appeal;
Let the edges of slaughter be sharp on their steel,
And the weight of destruction and swiftness of fear,
Speed death to his mark in their bullets' career!

Holy Nature, arise! from thy bosom in wrath
Shake the pestilence forth on the enemy's path,
That the tyrant invaders may march by the road
Of Sennacherib invading the city of God!

As the stars in their courses 'gainst Sisera strove,
Fight, mists of the fens, in the sick air above;
As Scamander his carcasses flung on the foe,
Fight, floods of the Theiss, in your torrents below!

As the snail of the Psalmist consuming away,
Let the moon-melted masses in silence decay;
Till the track of corruption alone in the air
Shall tell sicken'd Europe the Scythian was there!

Stay ! stay !—in thy fervour of sympathy pause,
Nor become inhumane in humanity's cause;
If the poor Russian slave have to wrong been
      abused,
Are the ties of Christ's brotherhood all to be loosed?

The mothers of Moscow who offer the breast
To their orphans, have hearts, as the mothers of
      Pest;
Nor are love's aspirations more tenderly drawn
From the bosoms of youth by the Theiss than the
      Don.

God of Russian and Magyar, who ne'er hast
      design'd
Save one shedding of blood for the sins of mankind,
No demon of battle and bloodshed art thou,
To the war-wearied nations be pitiful now !

Turn the hearts of the kings—let the Magyar again
Reap the harvests of peace on his bountiful plain;
And if not with renown, with affections and lives,
Send the driven serfs home to their children and
      wives !—

But you fill all my bosom with tumult once more—
What! Görgey surrender'd! What! Bem's battles
    o'er!
What! Haynau victorious!—Inscrutable God!
We must wonder, and worship, and bow to thy rod.

ADIEU TO BRITTANY.

RUGGED land of the granite and oak,
    I depart with a sigh from thy shore,
    And with kinsman's affection a blessing
  invoke
On the maids and the men of Arvôr.

For the Irish and Breton are kin,
    Though the lights of Antiquity pale
In the point of the dawn where the partings begin
    Of the Bolg, and the Kymro, and Gael.

But, though dim in the distance of time
    Be the low-burning beacons of fame,
Holy Nature attests us, in writing sublime
    On heart and on visage, the same.

In the dark-eye-lash'd eye of blue-grey,
　　In the open look, modest and kind,
In the face's fine oval reflecting the play
　　Of the sensitive, generous mind,

Till, as oft as by meadow and stream
　　With thy Maries and Josephs I roam,
In companionship gentle and friendly I seem,
　　As with Patrick and Brigid at home.

Green, meadow-fresh, streamy-bright land!
　　Though greener meads, valleys as fair,
Be at home, yet the home-yearning heart will demand,
　　Are they blest as in Brittany there?

Demand not—repining is vain:
　　Yet, would God, that even as thou
In thy homeliest homesteads, contented Bretagne,
　　Were the green isle my thoughts are with now!

But I call thee not golden: let gold
　　Deck the coronal troubadours twine,
Where the waves of the Loire and Garomna are
　　　　roll'd
　　Through the land of the white wheat and vine,

And the fire of the Frenchman goes up
   To the quick-thoughted, dark-flashing eye:
While Glory and Change quaffing Luxury's cup,
   Challenge all things below and on high.

Leave to him—to the vehement man
   Of the Loire, of the Seine, of the Rhone,—
In the Idea's high pathways to march in the van,
   To o'erthrow, and set up the o'erthrown:

Be it thine in the broad beaten ways
   That the world's simple seniors have trod,
To walk with soft steps, living peaceable days,
   And on earth not forgetful of God.

Nor repine that thy lot has been cast
   With the things of the old time before,
For to thee are committed the keys of the past,
   Oh grey monumental Arvôr!

Yes, land of the great Standing Stones,
   It is thine at thy feet to survey,
From thy earlier shepherd-kings' sepulchre-thrones
   The giant, far-stretching array;

Where, abroad o'er the górse-cover'd *lande*
  Where, along by the slow-breaking wave,
The hoary, inscrutable sentinels stand
  In their night-watch by History's grave.

Preserve them, nor fear for thy charge;
  From the prime of the morning they sprung,
When the works of young Mankind were lasting
      and large,
  As the will they embodied was young.

I have stood on Old Sarum:* the sun,
  With a pensive regard from the west,
Lit the beech-tops low down in the ditch of the
      Dun,
  Lit the service-trees high on its crest:

But the walls of the Roman were shrunk
  Into morsels of ruin around,
And palace of monarch, and minster of monk,
  Were effaced from the grassy-foss'd ground.

---

* *Sorbiodunum,* i.e. Service-tree-fort.

Like bubbles in ocean, they melt,
   O Wilts, on thy long-rolling plain,
And at last but the works of the hand of the Celt
   And the sweet hand of Nature remain.

Even so : though, portentous and strange,
   With a rumour of troublesome sounds,
On his iron way gliding, the Angel of Change
   Spread his dusky wings wide o'er thy bounds,—

He will pass : there'll be grass on his track,
   And the pick of the miner in vain
Shall search the dark void : while the stones of
      Carnac
   And the word of the Breton remain.

Farewell : up the waves of the Rance,
   See, we stream back our pennon of smoke ;
Farewell, russet skirt of the fine robe of France,
   Rugged land of the granite and oak !

WESTMINSTER ABBEY,

FROM England's gilded halls of state
 I cross'd the Western Minster's gate,
 And, 'mid the tombs of England's dead,
I heard the Holy Scriptures read.

The walls around and pillar'd piers
Had stood well-nigh seven hundred years;
The words the priest gave forth had stood
Since Christ, and since before the Flood.

A thousand hearts around partook
The comfort of the Holy Book;
Ten thousand suppliant hands were spread
In lifted stone above my head.

In dust decay'd the hands are gone
That fed and set the builders on;
In heedless dust the fingers lie
That hew'd and heav'd the stones on high;

And back to earth and air resolv'd
The brain that plann'd and pois'd the vault :—
But undecay'd, erect, and fair,
To heaven ascends the builded Prayer,

With majesty of strength and size,
With glory of harmonious dyes,
With holy airs of heavenward thought
From floor to roof divinely fraught.

Fall down, ye bars : enlarge, my soul !
To heart's content take in the whole;
And, spurning pride's injurious thrall,
With loyal love embrace them all !

Yet hold not lightly home; nor yet
The graves on Dunagore forget;
Nor grudge the stone-gilt stall to change
For humble bench of Gorman's Grange.

The self-same Word bestows its cheer
On simple creatures there as here;
And thence, as hence, poor souls do rise
In social flight to common skies.

For in the Presence vast and good,
That bends o'er all our livelihood,
With humankind in heavenly cure,
We all are like, we all are poor.

His poor, be sure, shall never want
For service meet or seemly chant,
And for the Gospel's joyful sound
A fitting place shall still be found;

Whether the organ's solemn tones
Thrill through the dust of warriors' bones,
Or voices of the village choir
From swallow-haunted eaves aspire,

Or, sped with healing on its wings,
The Word solicit ears of kings,
Or stir the souls, in moorland glen,
Of kingless covenanted men.

Enough for thee, indulgent Lord,
The willing ear to hear Thy Word,—
The rising of the burthen'd breast—
And thou suppliest all the rest.

VERSIONS AND ADAPTATIONS.

THE ORIGIN OF THE SCYTHIANS.

HERODOTUS ("MELPOMENE").

WHEN, o'er Riphæan wastes the son of
       Jove
    Slain Geryon's beeves from Erytheia
       drove,
Sharp nipp'd the frost, and feathery whirls of snow
Fill'd upper air and hid the earth below.
The hero on the ground, his steeds beside,
Spread, shaggy-huge, the dun Nemean hide,
And, warmly folded, while the tempest swept
The dreary Hyperborean desert, slept.

When Hercules awoke and look'd around,
The milk-white mares were nowhere to be found.
Long search'd the hero all the neighbouring plain,
The brakes and thickets; but he search'd in vain.

At length he reach'd a gloomy cave, and there
He found a woman as a goddess fair;
A perfect woman downward to the knee,
But all below, a snake, in coil'd deformity.

With mutual wonder each the other eyed:
He question'd of his steeds, and she replied:—
" Hero, thy steeds within my secret halls
Are safely stabled in enchanted stalls;
But if thou thence my captives wouldst remove,
Thou, captive too, must yield me love for love."

Won by the price, perchance by passion sway'd,
Alcides yielded to the monster maid.

The steeds recover'd, and the burnish'd car
Prepared, she said,—" Remember, when afar,
That, sprung from thee, three mighty sons shall
        prove
Me not unworthy of a hero's love.
But when my babes are grown to manhood, where
Would'st thou thy sons should seek a father's
        care ?"

The soft appeal e'en stern Alcides felt:—
And, " Take," he said, " this bow and glittering
      belt:"—
From his broad breast the baldrick he unslung,
(A golden phial from its buckle hung;)
" And, when my sons are grown to man's estate,
Him whom thou first shalt see decline the weight
Of the great belt, or fail the bow to bend,
To Theban Hercules, his father, send
For tutelage; but him whom thou shalt see
Thus bear the belt, thus bend the bow, like me,
Nought further needing by thy side retain,
The destined monarch of the northern plain."

He went: the mighty mother, at a birth,
Gave Gelon, Agathyrs and Scyth* to earth.
To early manhood grown, the former twain
Essay'd to bear the belt and bow in vain;
And, southward banish'd from their mother's
      face,
Sought lighter labours in the fields of Thrace:

---

  * In Celtic tradition, the progenitors of the Firbolgs, Picts,
and Scots respectively.

While, far refulgent over plain and wood,
Herculean Scyth the glittering belt indued,
And, striding dreadful on his fields of snow,
With aim unerring twang'd his father's bow.
From him derived, the illustrious Scythian name,
And all the race of Scythian monarchs came.

THE DEATH OF DERMID.

IRISH ROMANCE.

INTRODUCTORY NOTE.

ING CORMAC had affianced his daughter Grania to Finn, son of Comhal, the Finn Mac Coole of Irish, and Fingal of Scottish tradition. In addition to his warlike accomplishments, Finn was reported to have obtained the gifts of poetry, second-sight, and healing in the manner referred to below. On his personal introduction, his age and aspect proved displeasing to Grania, who threw herself on the gallantry of Dermid, the handsomest of Finn's attendant warriors, and induced him reluctantly to fly with her. Their pursuit by Finn forms the subject of one of the most popular native Irish romances. In the course of their wanderings, Dermid, having pursued a wild boar, met the fate of Adonis, who appears to have been his prototype in the Celtic imagination. Finn, arriving on the scene just before his rival's death, gives occasion to the most pathetic passage of the tale, which, at this point, is comparatively free from the characteristics of vulgarity and extravagance attaching to

the rest of the composition.   The incidents of the
original are followed in the piece below, which, however,
does not profess to be a translation.   The original may
be perused in the spirited version of Mr. O'Grady,—
" Publications of the Irish Ossianic Society," vol. iii.
p. 185.   It is from this Dermid that Highland tradition
draws the genealogy of the clan Campbell,—

   " The race of brown Dermid who slew the wild boar."

THE DEATH OF DERMID.

INN on the mountain found the mangled
                man,
         The slain boar by him.   " Dermid,"
      said the king,
" It likes me well at last to see thee thus.
This only grieves me, that the womankind
Of Erin are not also looking on :
Such sight were wholesome for the wanton eyes
So oft enamour'd of that specious form :
Beauty to foulness, strength to weakness turn'd."

" Yet in thy power, if only in thy will,
Lies it, oh Finn, even yet to heal me."

" How ?"

" Feign not the show of ignorance, nor deem
I know not of the virtues which thy hand
Drew from that fairy's half-discover'd hall,
Who bore her silver tankard from the fount,
So closely follow'd, that ere yet the door
Could close upon her steps, one arm was in ;
Wherewith, though seeing nought, yet touching all,
Thou grasped'st half the spiritual world ;
Withdrawing a heap'd handful of its gifts,—
Healing, and sight prophetic, and the power
Divine of poesy : but healing most
Abides within its hollow :—virtue such
That but so much of water as might wet
These lips, in that hand brought, would make me
          whole.
Finn, from the fountain fetch me in thy palms
A draught of water, and I yet shall live."

" How at these hands canst thou demand thy life,
Who took'st my joy of life ?"

            " She loved thee not:
Me she did love and doth; and were she here
She would so plead with thee that, for her sake,
Thou wouldst forgive us both, and bid me live."

" I was a man had spent my prime of years
In war and council, little bless'd with love;
Though poesy was mine, and, in my hour,
The seer's burthen not desirable;
And now at last had thought to have man's share
Of marriage blessings; and the King supreme,
Cormac, had pledged his only daughter mine;
When thou, with those pernicious beauty-gifts,
The flashing white tusk there hath somewhat
       spoil'd,
Didst win her to desert her father's house,
And roam the wilds with thee."

                " It was herself,
Grania, the Princess, put me in the bonds
Of holy chivalry to share her flight.
' Behold,' she said, ' he is an aged man,
(And so thou art, for years will come to all;)
And I, so young; and, at the Beltane games,

When Carbry Liffacher did play the men
Of Brea, I, unseen, saw thee snatch a hurl,
And thrice on Tara's champions* win the goal;
And gave thee love that day, and still will give.'
So she herself avow'd.   Resolve me, Finn,
For thou art just, could youthful warrior, sworn
To maiden's service, have done else than I?
No: hate me not—restore me—give me drink."

" I will not."

          " Nay, but, Finn, thou hadst not said
' I will not,' though I'd ask'd a greater boon,
That night we supp'd in Breendacoga's lodge.
Remember: we were faint and hunger-starved
From three day's flight; and even as on the board
They placed the viands, and my hand went forth
To raise the wine-cup, thou, more quick of ear,
O'erheard'st the stealthy leaguer set without;
And yet should'st eat or perish.   Then 'twas I,
Fasting, that made the sally; and 'twas I,
Fasting, that made the circuit of the court;

---

* " *On* Tara's champions," *ar ghasra Teamhrach.* The
idiom is preserved.

Three times I cours'd it, darkling, round and round ;
From whence returning, when I brought thee in
The three lopp'd heads of them that lurk'd without—
Thou hadst not then, refresh'd and grateful, said
' I will not,' had I ask'd thee, ' Give me drink.' "

" There springs no water on this summit bald."

" Nine paces from the spot thou standest on,
The well-eye—well thou knowest it—bubbles clear."

Abash'd, reluctant, to the bubbling well
Went Finn, and scoop'd the water in his palms ;
Wherewith returning, half-way, came the thought
Of Grania, and he let the water spill.

" Ah me," said Dermid, " hast thou then forgot
Thy warrior-art that oft, when helms were split,
And buckler-bosses shatter'd by the spear,
Has satisfied the thirst of wounded men ?
Ah, Finn, these hands of thine were not so slack
That night, when, captured by the king of Thule,
Thou layest in bonds within the temple gate
Waiting for morning, till the observant king

Should to his sun-god make thee sacrifice.
Close-pack'd thy fingers then, thong-drawn and
       squeezed,
The blood-drops oozing under every nail,
When, like a shadow, through the sleeping priests
Came I, and loos'd thee: and the hierophant
At day-dawn coming, on the altar-step,
Instead of victim straighten'd to his knife,
Two warriors found, erect, for battle arm'd."

Again abash'd, reluctant to the well
Went Finn, and scoop'd the water in his palms,
Wherewith returning, half-way, came the thought
That wrench'd him; and the shaken water spill'd.

" False one, thou didst it purposely! I swear
I saw thee, though mine eyes do fast grow dim.
Ah me, how much imperfect still is man!
Yet such were not the act of Him, whom once
On this same mountain, as we sat at eve—
Thou yet mayst see the knoll that was our couch,
A stone's throw from the spot where now I lie—
Thou showedst me, shuddering, when the seer's fit,
Sudden and cold as hail, assail'd thy soul

In vision of that Just One crucified
For all men's pardoning, which, once again,
Thou sawest, with Cormac, struck in Rossnaree."

Finn trembled; and a third time to the well
Went straight, and scoop'd the water in his palms;
Wherewith in haste half-way return'd, he saw
A smile on Dermid's face relax'd in death.

THE INVOCATION.

LUCRETIUS.

JOY of the world, divine delight of Love,
    Who with life-sowing footsteps soft dost
        move
Through all the still stars from their sliding stands
See, fishy seas, and fruit-abounding lands;
Bringing to presence of the gracious sun
All living things: thee blights and vapours shun,
And thine advent: for thee the various earth
Glows with the rose: for thee the murmurous mirth
Of ocean sparkles; and, at thy repair,
Diffusive bliss pervades the placid air.
For, see, forthwith the blandness of the Spring
Begins, and Zephyr's seasonable wing
Wantons abroad in primal lustihood,
Smit with sweet pangs the wing'd aerial brood

M

Of pairing birds proclaim thy reign begun;
Thence through the fields where pasturing cattle
      run,
Runs the soft frenzy, all the savage kind,
Touch'd with thy tremors in the wanton wind,
Prancing the plains, or through the rushing floods
Cleaving swift ways; thou, who through waving
      woods,
Tall mountains, fishful seas, and leafy bowers
Of nestling birds, keep'st up the joyous hours,
Making from age to age, bird, beast, and man
Perpetuate life and time;—aid thou my plan.

ARCHYTAS AND THE MARINER.

HORAT. OD. I. 28.

MARINER.

HEE, of the sea and land and unsumm'd
     sand
     The Mensurator,
The dearth of some poor earth from a friend's hand
     Detains, a waiter
For sepulture, here on the Matine strand;
     Nor aught the better
Art thou, Archytas, now, in thought to have spann'd
     Pole and equator!

ARCHYTAS.

The sire of Pelops, too, though guest and host
Of Gods, gave up the ghost:
     Beloved Tithonus into air withdrew:

And Minos, at the council-board of Jove
Once intimate above,

   Hell holds; and hell with strict embrace anew
Constrains Panthoïdes, for all his lore,
Though by the shield he bore

   In Trojan jousts, snatch'd from the trophied fane,
He testified that death slays nought within
The man, but nerve and skin;

   But bore his witness and his shield in vain.
For one night waits us all; one downward road
Must by all feet be trod:

   All heads at last to Proserpine must come:
The furious Fates to Mars's bloody shows
Cast these: the seas whelm those:

   Commix'd and close the young and old troop
      home.
Me also, prone Orion's comrade swift,
The South-wind, in the drift

   Of white Illyrian waves, caught from the day:
But, shipmate, thou refuse not to my dead
Bones and unburied head,

   The cheap poor tribute of the funeral clay!
So, whatsoe'er the East may foam or roar
Against the Hesperian shore,

   Let crack Venusia's woods, thou safe and free;

While great God Neptune, the Tarentine's trust,
And Jupiter the just,
　　With confluent wealth reward thy piety.
Ah! wouldst thou leave me? wouldst thou leave,
　　　　indeed,
Thy unoffending seed
　　Under the dead man's curse? Beware! the day
May come when thou shalt suffer equal wrong:
Give—'twill not keep thee long—
　　Three handfuls of sea-sand, and go thy way.

VERSIONS FROM THE IRISH.

VERSIONS FROM THE IRISH.

INTRODUCTORY NOTE.

N apology is needed for the rudeness of some of the following pieces. Irish poetical remains consist chiefly of bardic compositions and songs of the country, of which the examples here given could not be candidly rendered without some reflection of certain faults of the originals. The former class have inherent vices resulting from the conditions of their production. The office of the bard required skill in music, a retentive memory, and a knowledge of the common forms of panegyric, rather than original genius. A large proportion of these compositions consisted of adulatory odes addressed to protectors and patrons. Many of the best musical performances of Carolan are associated with words of this character, and exhibit an incongruous union of noble sounds and mean ideas. It has been usual, in giving him and the later harpers the credit which they well merit for originality and fertility in the production of melodies, to include their odes and songs, as efforts of poetic genius, in the commendation; but these portions of the compositions are generally made up of gross flatteries and the conventionalities of the Pantheon. The images and sentiments are in all much alike; and it is rarely that an original thought repays the trouble of the translator. In celebrating some of the ladies of families who patronized him, Carolan has, however, produced a few pieces in which the words are not unworthy of the music. He was sensible of the charms of grace and virtue, and although incapable of distinguishing between elegant and vulgar forms of praise, has in these instances expressed genuine sentiments of admiration with a great degree of natural and affectionate tenderness—united, it must be remembered, with original and beautiful music. One of these pieces, " Grace Nugent,"* although too full of the stock phrases of the adulatory school, is perhaps the most pleasing of its class. In addressing one of his male patrons also, in " The Cup of O'Hara,"† he exhibits some originality in transferring to his friend's wassail-cup the praises which were usually lavished on personal excellencies. It is among the country songs, however, that the greatest amount and variety of characteristic composition is found. In these we must not expect quite so much refinement as is found in the pieces composed by the bards and harpers, most of which have been transmitted in writing : for the

---

* See page 197.   † See page 201.

songs have only been preserved orally by the peasantry, who would naturally prefer such versions as suited their more homely tastes. If others of a more refined character have ever existed, they are not now forthcoming : but it is probable that at all times the songs of the native Irish have been of the same homely description as those which remain : for, before the introduction of English manners, there existed an almost complete personal equality among individuals of all ranks. It is still usual in some parts of the west of Ireland for the native population to use the Christian names of those to whom they speak, whatever may be the rank of the person addressed. These primitive manners admitted of but little difference in the modes of expressing ideas common to all; and, if we make a moderate allowance for the corruptions which most of these pieces have undergone in their transmission through more or less numerous generations of the populace, we shall probably be safe in taking them as approximate indexes of the tone and taste of native Irish society, in the castle as well as in the cabin. It has been the opinion of many judges in criticism that such a state of manners is the one most favourable to the development of the poetic faculty. Certainly, the lyrical pieces produced during such a phase of society afford a fuller insight into the humours and genius of a people than the offspring of any other period in its progress. It is not probable that the rural populace will ever again produce anything comparable to these effusions of a ruder age ; though the cultivated intellect and taste of the upper class, using the vehicle of a more copious though less fluent language, and applying itself to the wider range of ideas incident to an advanced state of civilization, may fairly hope to attain a much greater excellence: for, to say the truth, notwithstanding the strength of passion and abundance of sentiment and humour expressed in the country songs of the Irish, they have little vigour of thought and but a moderate degree of art in their structure: but not even the songs of Burns express sentiment more charmingly. Even in those dedicated to festivity and the chase, a sweet and delicate pathos mingles with the ordinary topics, which it is as difficult to catch in translation, as it is in music to define or analyse the characteristic tones and turns of the melody. The general structure of the melody is, with few exceptions, the same in all. A writer to whom Ireland is largely indebted in almost all the departments of art and literature, Dr. Petrie, thus describes their peculiar arrangement. " They are formed, for the most part, of four strains of equal length. The first soft, pathetic, and subdued; the second ascends in the scale, and becomes bold, energetic, and impassioned; the third, a repetition of the second, is sometimes a little varied and more florid, and leads, often by a graceful or melancholy passage, to the fourth, which is always a repetition of the first." The same writer has beautifully and truly compared the effect of the last part following the bold and surcharged strains of the second and third, to the dissolution in genial showers of a summer cloud.

This progress of the melody is often reflected in the structure of the song, which, beginning plaintively and tenderly mounts with the music in vehemence, and subsides with it in renewed tenderness at the conclusion of the stanza.   This analogy between the sentiment and melody runs through many of the following pieces, as, for example, the *naïve* and rustic but tender song of " The Coolun,"* and may be observed in the passionate old strain " Cean Dubh Deelish,"† where the energy of the middle part of the piece is also associated with one of those duplications of the rhythm which constitute a peculiar characteristic of Irish song-writing. It is difficult in English to imitate these duplications and crassitudes, which give so much of its effect to the original, where, owing to the pliancy of the sounds, several syllables are often, as it were, fused together, and internal rhymes and correspondences produced within the body of the line : such as, for example, in " The Boatman."‡

Oh Whillan, rough, bold-faced rock, that stoop'st o'er the bay,
Look forth at the new barque beneath me cleaving her way ;
Saw ye ever, on sea or river, 'mid the mounting of spray,
Boat made of a tree that urges through the surges like mine to-day,
On the tide-top, the tide-top?

" I remember," says Whillan, " a rock I have ever been ;
And constant my watch, each day, o'er the sea-wave green ;
But of all that I ever of barques and of galleys have seen,
This that urges through the surges beneath you to-day is queen
On the tide-top, the tide-top."

---

* See page 211.   † See page 216.   ‡ See page 217.

It is a significant fact that some of the best of the native amatory songs appear to have been the compositions of men in outlawry and in misery. In the " County Leitrim," the fear of famine mingles with the ardour of desire ; and scarcity and poverty enter largely into the sentiment of " Cashel of Munster."* A large number also of this class of compositions are songs of humble life. Some of these, such as " Youghall Harbour,"† despite the rusticity of the topics, bespeak much generous feeling and sensibility ; and, as regards all, the observation may be made that they are wedded to strains of music wonderfully various, expressive, and sweet to native ears. The production either of melodies or of accompanying words has now wholly ceased ; and the language itself, within another generation, will probably be no longer spoken in Ireland.

---

* See page 209. † See page 214.

DEIRDRA'S FAREWELL TO ALBA.

OLD IRISH ROMANCE.*

FAREWELL to fair Alba, high house of
  the sun,
  Farewell to the mountain, the cliff, and
  the dun;
Dun Sweeny adieu! for my love cannot stay,
And tarry I may not when love cries away.

Glen Vashan! Glen Vashan! where roebucks run
  free,
Where my love used to feast on the red deer with
  me,
Where rock'd on thy waters while stormy winds
  blew,
My love used to slumber, Glen Vashan adieu!

---

 * The tale of the tragical fate of the sons of Usnach, from
which this and the following piece have been taken, may be
seen in the " Transactions of the Iberno-Celtic Society,"
Dublin, 1808; and in the " Atlantis," Dublin, 1860.

Glendaro! Glendaro! where birchen boughs weep
Honey dew at high noon o'er the nightingale's sleep,
Where my love used to lead me to hear the cuckoo
'Mong the high hazel bushes, Glendaro, adieu!

Glen Urchy! Glen Urchy! where loudly and long
My love used to wake up the woods with his song,
While the son of the rock,* from the depths of the
          dell,
Laugh'd sweetly in answer, Glen Urchy, farewell!

Glen Etive! Glen Etive! where dappled does
          roam,
Where I leave the green sheeling I first call'd a
          home;
Where with me and my true love delighted to dwell,
The sun made his mansion, Glen Etive, farewell!

Farewell to Inch Draynach, adieu to the roar
Of the blue billows bursting in light on the shore;
Dun Fiagh, farewell! for my love cannot stay,
And tarry I may not when love cries away.

---

* *Son of the rock,* i. e. Echo.

DEIRDRA'S LAMENT FOR THE SONS OF USNACH.

OLD IRISH ROMANCE.

THE lions of the hill are gone,
And I am left alone—alone—
Dig the grave both wide and deep,
For I am sick, and fain would sleep!

The falcons of the wood are flown,
And I am left alone—alone—
Dig the grave both deep and wide,
And let us slumber side by side.

The dragons of the rock are sleeping,
Sleep that wakes not for our weeping:
Dig the grave, and make it ready;
Lay me on my true-love's body.

N

Lay their spears and bucklers bright
By the warriors' sides aright;
Many a day the three before me
On their linked bucklers bore me.

Lay upon the low grave floor,
'Neath each head, the blue claymore;
Many a time the noble three
Redden'd these blue blades for me.

Lay the collars, as is meet,
Of their greyhounds at their feet;
Many a time for me have they
Brought the tall red deer to bay.

In the falcon's jesses throw,
Hook and arrow, line and bow;
Never again by stream or plain
Shall the gentle woodsmen go.

Sweet companions ye were ever—
Harsh to me, your sister, never;
Woods and wilds and misty valleys
Were, with you, as good's a palace.

Oh ! to hear my true love singing,
Sweet as sound of trumpets ringing :
Like the sway of ocean swelling
Roll'd his deep voice round our dwelling.

Oh ! to hear the echoes pealing
Round our green and fairy sheeling,
When the three, with soaring chorus,
Pass'd the silent skylark o'er us.

Echo now, sleep, morn and even—
Lark alone enchant the heaven !—
Ardan's lips are scant of breath,
Neesa's tongue is cold in death.

Stag, exult on glen and mountain—
Salmon, leap from loch to fountain—
Heron, in the free air warm ye—
Usnach's sons no more will harm ye !

Erin's stay no more you are,
Rulers of the ridge of war ;
Never more 'twill be your fate
To keep the beam of battle straight !

Woe is me ! by fraud and wrong,
Traitors false and tyrants strong,
Fell clan Usnach, bought and sold,
For Barach's feast and Conor's gold !

Woe to Eman, roof and wall !—
Woe to Red Branch, hearth and hall !—
Tenfold woe and black dishonour
To the foul and false clan Conor !

Dig the grave both wide and deep,
Sick I am, and fain would sleep !
Dig the grave and make it ready,
Lay me on my true-love's body !

THE DOWNFALL OF THE GAEL.

O'GNIVE,* BARD OF O'NEILL.

Cir. 1580.

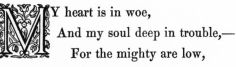Y heart is in woe,
And my soul deep in trouble,—
For the mighty are low,
And abased are the noble:

The Sons of the Gael
Are in exile and mourning,
Worn, weary, and pale,
As spent pilgrims returning;

Or men who, in flight
From the field of disaster,
Beseech the black night
On their flight to fall faster;

---

* O'Gnive, now Agnew.

Or seamen aghast
When their planks gape asunder,
And the waves fierce and fast
Tumble through in hoarse thunder;

Or men whom we see
That have got their death-omen—
Such wretches are we
In the chains of our foemen!

Our courage is fear,
Our nobility vileness,
Our hope is despair,
And our comeliness foulness.

There is mist on our heads,
And a cloud chill and hoary
Of black sorrow, sheds
An eclipse on our glory.

From Boyne to the Linn
Has the mandate been given,
That the children of Finn
From their country be driven.

That the sons of the king—
Oh, the treason and malice!—
  Shall no more ride the ring
In their own native valleys;

  No more shall repair
Where the hill foxes tarry,
  Nor forth to the air
Fling the hawk at her quarry:

  For the plain shall be broke
By the share of the stranger,
  And the stone-mason's stroke
Tell the woods of their danger;

  The green hills and shore
Be with white keeps disfigured,
  And the Mote of Rathmore
Be the Saxon churl's haggard!

  The land of the lakes
Shall no more know the prospect
  Of valleys and brakes—
So transform'd is her aspect!

The Gael cannot tell,
In the uprooted wild-wood
  And red ridgy dell,
The old nurse of his childhood :

  The nurse of his youth
Is in doubt as she views him,
  If the wan wretch, in truth,
Be the child of her bosom.

  We starve by the board,
And we thirst amid wassail—
  For the guest is the lord,
And the host is the vassal !

  Through the woods let us roam,
Through the wastes wild and barren ;
  We are strangers at home !
We are exiles in Erin !

  And Erin's a bark
O'er the wide waters driven !
  And the tempest howls dark,
And her side planks are riven !

And in billows of might
Swell the Saxon before her,—
Unite, oh, unite!
Or the billows burst o'er her!

O'BYRNE'S BARD TO THE CLANS OF WICKLOW.

Cir. 1580.

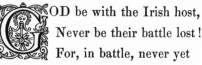

GOD be with the Irish host,
Never be their battle lost!
For, in battle, never yet
Have they basely earn'd defeat.

Host of armour red and bright,
May ye fight a valiant fight!
For the green spot of the earth,
For the land that gave you birth.

Who in Erin's cause would stand,
Brothers of the avenging band,
He must wed immortal quarrel,
Pain and sweat and bloody peril.

On the mountain bare and steep,
Snatching short but pleasant sleep,
Then, ere sunrise, from his eyrie,
Swooping on the Saxon quarry.

What although you've fail'd to keep
Liffey's plain or Tara's steep,
Cashel's pleasant streams to save,
Or the meads of Croghan Maev;

Want of conduct lost the town,
Broke the white-wall'd castle down,
Moira lost, and old Taltin,
And let the conquering stranger in.

'Twas the want of right command,
Not the lack of heart or hand,
Left your hills and plains to-day
'Neath the strong Clan Saxon's sway.

Ah, had heaven never sent
Discord for our punishment,
Triumphs few o'er Erin's host
Had Clan London now to boast!

Woe is me, 'tis God's decree
Strangers have the victory:
Irishmen may now be found
Outlaws upon Irish ground.

Like a wild beast in his den
Lies the chief by hill and glen,
While the strangers, proud and savage,
Criffan's richest valleys ravage.

Woe is me, the foul offence,
Treachery and violence,
Done against my people's rights—
Well may mine be restless nights!

When old Leinster's sons of fame,
Heads of many a warlike name,
Redden their victorious hilts
On the Gaul, my soul exults.

When the grim Gaul, who have come
Hither o'er the ocean foam,
From the fight victorious go,
Then my heart sinks deadly low.

Bless the blades our warriors draw,
God be with Clan Ranelagh!
But my soul is weak for fear,
Thinking of their danger here.

Have them in thy holy eeping,
God be with them lying sleeping,
God be with them standing fighting,
Erin's foes in battle smiting!

LAMENT OVER THE RUINS OF THE ABBEY OF TIMOLEAGUE.

JOHN COLLINS, died, 1816.

LONE and weary as I wander'd
      By the bleak shore of the sea,
      Meditating and reflecting
  On the world's hard destiny;

Forth the moon and stars 'gan glimmer,
  In the quiet tide beneath,—
For on slumbering spray and blossom
  Breathed not out of heaven a breath.

On I went in sad dejection,
  Careless where my footsteps bore,
Till a ruin'd church before me
  Open'd wide its ancient door,—

Till I stood before the portals,
  Where of old were wont to be,
For the blind, the halt, and leper,
  Alms and hospitality.

Still the ancient seat was standing,
  Built against the buttress grey,
Where the clergy used to welcome
  Weary travellers on their way.

There I sat me down in sadness,
  'Neath my cheek I placed my hand,
Till the tears fell hot and briny
  Down upon the grassy land.

There, I said in woeful sorrow,
  Weeping bitterly the while,
Was a time when joy and gladness
  Reign'd within this ruin'd pile;—

Was a time when bells were tinkling,
  Clergy preaching peace abroad,
Psalms a-singing, music ringing
  Praises to the mighty God.

Empty aisle, deserted chancel,
   Tower tottering to your fall,
Many a storm since then has beaten
   On the grey head of your wall!

Many a bitter storm and tempest
   Has your roof-tree turn'd away,
Since you first were form'd a temple
   To the Lord of night and day.

Holy house of ivied gables,
   That wert once the country's pride,
Houseless now in weary wandering
   Roam your inmates far and wide.

Lone you are to-day, and dismal,—
   Joyful psalms no more are heard
Where, within your choir, her vesper
   Screeches the cat-headed bird.

Ivy from your eaves is growing,
   Nettles round your green hearth-stone,
Foxes howl, where, in your corners,
   Dropping waters make their moan.

Where the lark to early matins
   Used your clergy forth to call,
There, alas! no tongue is stirring,
   Save the daw's upon the wall.

Refectory cold and empty,
   Dormitory bleak and bare,
Where are now your pious uses,
   Simple bed and frugal fare?

Gone your abbot, rule and order,
   Broken down your altar stones;
Nought see I beneath your shelter,
   Save a heap of clayey bones.

Oh! the hardship, oh! the hatred,
   Tyranny, and cruel war,
Persecution and oppression,
   That have left you as you are!

I myself once also prosper'd;—
   Mine is, too, an alter'd plight;
Trouble, care, and age have left me
   Good for nought but grief to-night.

o

Gone, my motion and my vigour,—
  Gone, the use of eye and ear;
At my feet lie friends and children,
  Powerless and corrupting here:

Woe is written on my visage,
  In a nut my heart would lie—
Death's deliverance were welcome—
  Father, let the old man die.

TO THE HARPER O'CONNELLAN.

ENCHANTER who reignest
　　Supreme o'er the North,
　　Who hast wiled the coy spirit
　Of true music forth ;
In vain Europe's minstrels
　To honour aspire,
When thy swift slender fingers
　Go forth on the wire !

There is no heart's desire
　Can be felt by a king,
That thy hand cannot match
　From the soul of the string,
By its conquering, capturing,
　Magical sway,
For, charmer, thou stealest
　Thy notes from a fay !

Enchanter, I say,—
   For thy magical skill
Can soothe every sorrow,
   And heal every ill:
Who hear thee they praise thee;
   They weep while they praise;
For, charmer, from Fairyland
   Fresh are thy lays!

GRACE NUGENT.

CAROLAN.

BRIGHTEST blossom of the Spring,
　Grace, the sprightly girl I sing:
　Grace, who bore the palm of mind
From all the rest of womankind.
Whomsoe'er the fates decree,
Happy fate! for life to be
Day and night my Coolun near,
Ache or pain need never fear!

Her neck outdoes the stately swan,
Her radiant face the summer dawn:
Ah, happy thrice the youth for whom
The fates design that branch of bloom!
Pleasant are your words benign,
　Rich those azure eyes of thine:
Ye who see my queen, beware
Those twisted links of golden hair!

This is what I fain would say
To the bird-voiced lady gay,—
Never yet conceived the heart
Joy which Grace cannot impart:
Fold of jewels ! case of pearls !
Coolun of the circling curls !
More I say not, but no less
Drink you health and happiness !

MILD MABEL KELLY.

CAROLAN.

WHOEVER the youth who, by Heaven's
  decree
  Has his happy right hand 'neath that
   bright head of thine,
 'Tis certain that he
 From all sorrow is free
Till the day of his death, if a life so divine
Should not raise him in bliss above mortal degree:
Mild Mabel-ni-Kelly, bright Coolun of curls,
 All stately and pure as the swan on the lake;
Her mouth of white teeth is a palace of pearls,
 And the youth of the land are love-sick for her
  sake!

No strain of the sweetest e'er heard in the land
 That she knows not to sing, in a voice so en-
  chanting,

That the cranes on the strand
Fall asleep where they stand;
Oh, for her blooms the rose, and the lily ne'er
wanting
To shed its mild radiance o'er bosom or hand:
The dewy blue blossom that hangs on the spray,
More blue than her eye, human eye never saw,
Deceit never lurk'd in its beautiful ray,—
Dear lady, I drink to you, *slainte go bragh!*

THE CUP OF O'HARA.

CAROLAN.

WERE I west in green Arran,
   Or south in Glanmore,
   Where the long ships come laden
With claret in store;
Yet I'd rather than shiploads
   Of claret, and ships,
Have your white cup, O'Hara,
   Up full at my lips.

But why seek in numbers
   Its virtues to tell,
When O'Hara's own chaplain
   Has said, saying well,—
" Turlogh,* bold son of Brian,
   Sit ye down, boy, again,
Till we drain the great *cupaun*
   In another health to Keane."†

---

* Turlogh Carolan, the composer.
† Keane O'Hara, the patron.

THE FAIR-HAIR'D GIRL.

IRISH SONG.

THE sun has set, the stars are still,
The red moon hides behind the hill;
The tide has left the brown beach bare,
The birds have fled the upper air;
Upon her branch the lone cuckoo
Is chaunting still her sad adieu;
And you, my fair-hair'd girl, must go
Across the salt sea under woe!

I through love have learn'd three things,
Sorrow, sin, and death it brings;
Yet day by day my heart within
Dares shame and sorrow, death and sin:
Maiden, you have aim'd the dart
Rankling in my ruin'd heart:
Maiden, may the God above
Grant you grace to grant me love!

Sweeter than the viol's string,
And the notes that blackbirds sing;
Brighter than the dewdrops rare
Is the maiden wondrous fair:
Like the silver swans at play
Is her neck, as bright as day!
Woe is me, that e'er my sight
Dwelt on charms so deadly bright!

PASTHEEN FINN.

IRISH RUSTIC SONG.

OH, my fair Pastheen is my heart's de-
light,
Her gay heart laughs in her blue eye
bright;
Like the apple blossom her bosom white,
And her neck like the swan's, on a March morn
bright!
Then, Oro, come with me! come with me!
come * with me!
Oro, come with me! brown girl, sweet!
And, oh! I would go through snow and sleet,
If you would come with me, brown girl,
sweet!

Love of my heart, my fair Pastheen!
Her cheeks are red as the rose's sheen,

---

* The emphasis is on " come."

But my lips have tasted no more, I ween,
Than the glass I drank to the health of my queen!
    Then, Oro, come with me! come with me!
      come with me!
    Oro, come with me! brown girl, sweet!
    And, oh! I would go through snow and sleet,
    If you would come with me, brown girl,
      sweet!

Were I in the town, where's mirth and glee,
Or 'twixt two barrels of barley bree,
With my fair Pastheen upon my knee,
'Tis I would drink to her pleasantly!
    Then, Oro, come with me! come with me!
      come with me!
    Oro, come with me! brown girl, sweet!
    And, oh! I would go through snow and sleet,
    If you would come with me, brown girl,
      sweet!

Nine nights I lay in longing and pain,
Betwixt two bushes, beneath the rain,

Thinking to see you, love, once again;
But whistle and call were all in vain!

    Then, Oro, come with me! come with me!
        come with me!
    Oro, come with me! brown girl, sweet!
    And, oh! I would go through snow and sleet,
    If you would come with me, brown girl,
        sweet!

I'll leave my people, both friend and foe;
From all the girls in the world I'll go;
But from you, sweetheart, oh, never! oh, no!
'Till I lie in the coffin, stretch'd cold and low!

    Then, Oro, come with me! come with me!
        come with me!
    Oro, come with me! brown girl, sweet!
    And, oh! I would go through snow and sleet,
    If you would come with me, brown girl,
        sweet!

MOLLY ASTORE.

IRISH SONG.

OH, Mary dear, oh, Mary fair,
    Oh, branch of generous stem,
    White blossom of the banks of Nair,
  Though lilies grow on them!
You've left me sick at heart for love,
  So faint I cannot see,
The candle swims the board above,
  I'm drunk for love of thee!
Oh, stately stem of maiden pride,
  My woe it is, and pain,
That I, thus sever'd from thy side,
  The long night must remain!

Through all the towns of Innisfail
  I've wander'd far and wide;
But from Downpatrick to Kinsale,
  From Carlow to Kilbride,

'Mong lords and dames of high degree,
  Where'er my feet have gone,
My Mary, one to equal thee
  I've never look'd upon;
I live in darkness and in doubt
  Whene'er my love's away,
But, were the blessed sun put out,
  Her shadow would make day !

'Tis she indeed, young bud of bliss,
  And gentle as she's fair,
Though lily-white her bosom is,
  And sunny-bright her hair,
And dewy-azure her blue eye,
  And rosy-red her cheek,—
Yet brighter she in modesty,
  More beautifully meek !
The world's wise men from north to south
  Can never cure my pain;
But one kiss from her honey mouth
  Would make me whole again !

CASHEL OF MUNSTER.

IRISH RUSTIC BALLAD.

'D wed you without herds, without money,
or rich array,
And I'd wed you on a dewy morning at
day-dawn grey;
My bitter woe it is, love, that we are not far away
In Cashel town, though the bare deal board were
our marriage-bed this day!

Oh, fair maid, remember the green hill side,
Remember how I hunted about the valleys wide;
Time now has worn me; my locks are turn'd to
grey,
The year is scarce and I am poor, but send me not,
love, away!

Oh, deem not my blood is of base strain, my girl,
Oh, deem not my birth was as the birth of the churl;

F

Marry me, and prove me, and say soon you will,
That noble blood is written on my right side still!

My purse holds no red gold, no coin of the silver
    white,
No herds are mine to drive through the long twi-
    light!
But the pretty girl that would take me, all bare
    though I be and lone,
Oh, I'd take her with me kindly to the county
    Tyrone.

Oh, my girl, I can see 'tis in trouble you are,
And, oh, my girl, I see 'tis your people's reproach
    you bear:
" I am a girl in trouble for his sake with whom I fly,
And, oh, may no other maiden know such reproach
    as I!"

THE COOLUN.

H, had you seen the Coolun,
  Walking down by the cuckoo's street,
  With the dew of the meadow shining
On her milk-white twinkling feet.
My love she is, and my *coleen oge*,
  And she dwells in Bal'nagar;
And she bears the palm of beauty bright
  From the fairest that in Erin are.

In Bal'nagar is the Coolun,
  Like the berry on the bough her cheek;
Bright beauty dwells for ever
  On her fair neck and ringlets sleek:
Oh, sweeter is her mouth's soft music
  Than the lark or thrush at dawn,
Or the blackbird in the greenwood singing
  Farewell to the setting sun.

Rise up, my boy ! make ready
   My horse, for I forth would ride,
To follow the modest damsel,
   Where she walks on the green hill side :
For, ever since our youth were we plighted,
   In faith, troth, and wedlock true—
She is sweeter to me nine times over
   Than organ or cuckoo !

For, ever since my childhood
   I loved the fair and darling child ;
But our people came between us,
   And with lucre our pure love defiled :
Oh, my woe it is, and my bitter pain,
   And I weep it night and day,
That the *coleen bawn* of my early love
   Is torn from my heart away.

Sweetheart and faithful treasure,
   Be constant still, and true ;
Nor for want of herds and houses
   Leave one who would ne'er leave you :
I'll pledge you the blessed Bible,
   Without and eke within,

That the faithful God will provide for us,
Without thanks to kith or kin.

Oh, love, do you remember
When we lay all night alone,
Beneath the ash in the winter-storm,
When the oak wood round did groan?
No shelter then from the blast had we,
The bitter blast or sleet,
But your gown to wrap about our heads,
And my coat round our feet.

YOUGHALL HARBOUR.

IRISH RUSTIC BALLAD.

ONE sunday morning, into Youghall
    walking,
      I met a maiden upon the way;
Her little mouth sweet as fairy music,
    Her soft cheeks blushing like dawn of day!
I laid a bold hand upon her bosom,
    And ask'd a kiss: but she answer'd, " No:
Fair sir, be gentle; do not tear my mantle;
    'Tis none in Erin my grief can know.

" 'Tis but a little hour since I left Youghall,
    And my love forbade me to return;
And now my weary way I wander
    Into Cappoquin, a poor girl forlorn:
Then do not tempt me; for, alas! I dread them
    Who with tempting proffers teach girls to roam,
Who'd first deceive us, then faithless leave us,
    And send us shame-faced and bare-foot home."

" My heart and hand here! I mean you marriage!
    I have loved like you and known love's pain ;
And if you turn back now to Youghall Harbour,
    You ne'er shall want house or home again :
You shall have a lace cap like any lady,
    Cloak and capuchin, too, to keep you warm,
And if God please, maybe, a little baby,
    By and bye, to nestle within your arm."

CEAN DUBH DEELISH.*

PUT your head, darling, darling, darling,
    Your darling black head my heart
      above;
Oh, mouth of honey, with the thyme for fragrance,
  Who, with heart in breast, could deny you love?
Oh, many and many a young girl for me is pining,
  Letting her locks of gold to the cold wind free,
For me, the foremost of our gay young fellows;
  But I'd leave a hundred, pure love, for thee!
Then put your head, darling, darling, darling,
  Your darling black head my heart above;
Oh, mouth of honey, with the thyme for fragrance,
  Who, with heart in breast, could deny you love?

---

* Pronounced *Cawn dhu deelish*, i.e., dear black head.

BOATMAN'S HYMN.

BARK that bear me through foam and
squall,
You in the storm are my castle wall:
Though the sea should redden from bottom to top,
From tiller to mast she takes no drop;
    On the tide-top, the tide-top,
        Wherry *aroon*, my land and store!
    On the tide-top, the tide-top,
        She is the boat can sail *go leor*.*

She dresses herself, and goes gliding on,
Like a dame in her robes of the Indian lawn;
For God has bless'd her, gunnel and whale,
And oh! if you saw her stretch out to the gale,
    On the tide-top, the tide-top, &c.

Whillan,† ahoy! old heart of stone,
Stooping so black o'er the beach alone,

---

* *go leor*, i e. abundantly well.
† Whillan, a rock on the shore near Blacksod Harbour.

Answer me well—on the bursting brine
Saw you ever a bark like mine?
  On the tide-top, the tide-top, &c.

Says Whillan,—" Since first I was made of stone,
I have look'd abroad o'er the beach alone—
But till to-day, on the bursting brine,
Saw I never a bark like thine,"
  On the tide-top, the tide-top, &c.

" God of the air!" the seamen shout,
When they see us tossing the brine about:
" Give us the shelter of strand or rock,
Or through and through us she goes with a shock!"
  On the tide-top, the tide-top,
    Wherry *aroon*, my land and store,
  On the tide-top, the tide-top,
    She is the boat can sail *go leor!*

THE DEAR OLD AIR.

MISFORTUNE'S train may chase our
   joys,
  But not our love;
And I those pensive looks will prize,
  The smiles of joy above:
Your tender looks of love shall still
  Delight and console;
Even though your eyes the tear-drops fill
  Beyond your love's control.

Of troubles past we will not speak,
  Or future woe:
Nor mark, thus leaning cheek to cheek,
  The stealing tear-drops flow:
But I'll sing you the dear old Irish air,
  Soothing and low,
You loved so well when, gay as fair,
  You won me long ago.

THE LAPFUL OF NUTS.

WHENE'ER I see soft hazel eyes
    And nut-brown curls,
    I think of those bright days I spent
  Among the Limerick girls;
When up through Cratla woods I went,
    Nutting with thee;
And we pluck'd the glossy clustering fruit
  From many a bending tree.

Beneath the hazel boughs we sat,
    Thou, love, and I,
And the gather'd nuts lay in thy lap,
    Beneath thy downcast eye:
But little we thought of the store we'd won,
    I, love, or thou;
For our hearts were full, and we dare not own
  The love that's spoken now.

Oh, there's wars for willing hearts in Spain,
  And high Germanie!
And I'll come back, ere long, again,
  With knightly fame and fee:
And I'll come back, if I ever come back,
  Faithful to thee,
That sat with thy white lap full of nuts
  Beneath the hazel tree.

MARY'S WAKING.

SOFT be the sleep, and sweet the dreams,
    And bright be the awaking,
  Of Mary this mild April morn,
    On my pale vigil breaking:
May weariness and wakefulness
    And unrepaid endeavour,
And aching eyes like mine this day,
    Be far from her for ever!

The quiet of the opening dawn,
    The freshness of the morning,
Be with her through the cheerful day,
    Till peaceful eve returning
Shall put an end to household cares
    And dutiful employment,
And bring the hours of genial mirth
    And innocent enjoyment.

And whether in the virgin choir,
    A joyous sylph, she dances,

Or o'er the smiling circle sheds
    Her wit's sweet influences ;
May he by favouring fate assign'd
    Her partner or companion,
Be one that with an angel's mind
    Is fit to hold communion.

Ah me ! the wish is hard to frame !
    But should some youth, more favour'd,
Achieve the happiness which I
    Have fruitlessly endeavour'd,
God send them love and length of days,
    And health and wealth abounding,
And long around their hearth to hear
    Their children's voices sounding !

Be still, be still, rebellious heart;
    If he have fairly won her,
To bless their union I am bound
    In duty and in honour :
But, out alas ! 'tis all in vain ;
    I love her still too dearly
To pray for blessings which I feel
    So hard to give sincerely.

HOPELESS LOVE.

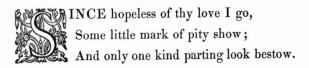

INCE hopeless of thy love I go,
 Some little mark of pity show;
 And only one kind parting look bestow.

One parting look of pity mild
On him, through starless tempest wild,
Who lonely hence to-night must go, exiled.

But even rejected love can warm
The heart through night and storm:
And unrelenting though they be,
Thine eyes beam life on me.

And I will bear that look benign
Within this darkly-troubled breast to shine,
Though never, never can thyself, ah me, be mine!

THE FAIR HILLS OF IRELAND.

OLD IRISH SONG.

PLENTEOUS place is Ireland for hos-
      pitable cheer,
      Uileacan dubh O !
Where the wholesome fruit is bursting from the
      yellow barley ear;
      Uileacan dubh O !
There is honey in the trees where her misty vales
      expand,
And her forest paths, in summer, are by falling
      waters fann'd,
There is dew at high noontide there, and springs
      i'the yellow sand,
  On the fair hills of holy Ireland.

Curl'd he is and ringletted, and plaited to the
      knee,
      Uileacan dubh O !

Q

Each captain who comes sailing across the Irish
　　sea;
　　　　　Uileacan dubh O !
And I will make my journey, if life and health but
　　stand,
Unto that pleasant country, that fresh and fragrant
　　strand,
And leave your boasted braveries, your wealth and
　　high command,
　For the fair hills of holy Ireland.

Large and profitable are the stacks upon the ground,
　　　　Uileacan dubh O !
The butter and the cream do wondrously abound,
　　　　Uileacan dubh O !
The cresses on the water and the sorrels are at hand,
And the cuckoo's calling daily his note of music
　　bland,
And the bold thrush sings so bravely his song i'the
　　forests grand,
　On the fair hills of holy Ireland.

NOTES.

NOTES.

1. Page 6. *" Giving aught the bard demanded."*

THE exactions of the bards were so intolerable, that the early Irish more than once endeavoured to rid themselves of the order, but without success. The *Aeir* or satire of the bard was deemed an instrument of physical mischief, capable of destroying the life and property, as well as the peace of mind, of the person against whom it was directed. Rather than incur its terrors, the early Irish submitted to bardic exactions which would appear incredible, if we did not know that even within the present generation the same belief in the power of the *Bhat* (*vates*) existed in the East.

2. Page 7. *" Tara Luachra's hall."*

The seat of the early kings of West Munster, in the mountainous region of Desmond, site unknown : the scene of a session of the bards in the Sixth, and of an exploit similar to the burning of Persepolis (*magna componere parvis*), by Cuchullin and the Companions of the Red Branch, in a fit of intoxication, in the First Century.

3. Page 8. *" The hither Gael."*

Iar-Gael—*Argyle.*

4. Page 8. " *The cauldron-pool of Brecan.*"

Corrievreakan, the *maelstrom* of the Orcades. Like other famous whirlpools, it no longer answers to the ancient account of its terrors. The picturesque force of the description in Cormac's Glossary is enhanced by our inability to translate the whole of some of the similes.

" *Coire-Brecain*, i. e., a great vortex between Ere and Alba to the north, i. e., the conflux of the different seas, viz., the sea which encompasses Ere at the north-west, the sea which encompasses Alba at the north-west, and the sea to the south, between Ere and Alba. They rush at each other after the likeness of a *luaithrinde*, and each is buried into the other like the *oircel tairechta*, and they are sucked down into the gulph so as to form a gaping cauldron, which would receive all Ere into its wide mouth. The waters are again thrown up, so that their belching, roaring, and thundering are heard amid the clouds, and they boil like a cauldron upon a fire."

5. Page 8. " *The stone fort of Dun-Britan.*"

Dunbarton, formerly *Ail-Clyde*, the stone fort of the Clyde.

6. Page 9. " *Where the whitening surges spread below the Herdsman Hill.*"

A feeble effort to convey something of the solitary grandeur of the valley around Loch Etive. Had M'Culloch known the details of the noble romance, the traces of which he still found surviving in this retreat of the sons of Usnach, it might have added something to his own enjoyment of the scene, but it could not have increased the impressiveness of his description. " There is a gigantic simplicity about the whole scene, which would render the presence of these objects and of that variety which constitute picturesque beauty, intrusive and impertinent. I know not if Loch Etive could bear an ornament without an infringement on that aspect of solitary vastness which it presents throughout; nor is there one. The rocks and bays on the shore, which might else-where attract attention, are here swallowed up in the enormous dimensions of the surrounding mountains, and the wide and simple expanse of the lake. Here also, as at Loch Coruisk and Glen Sanicks, we experience the effect arising from simplicity of form. At the first view, the whole expanse appears comprised within a mile or two; nor is it until we find the extremity still remote and misty as we advance, and the aspect of everything remaining unchanged, that we begin to feel and comprehend the vast and overwhelming magnitude of all around. It is hence also, perhaps, as in that singular valley (Glen Sanicks) that there is here that sense of eternal silence and repose, as if in this spot creation had for ever slept. The billows that are seen whitening the shore are inaudible, the cascade pours down the declivity unheard, and the clouds are hurried along the tops of the mountains before the blast, but no sound of the storm reaches the ear. There is some-thing in the colouring of this spot which is equally singular, and which adds much to the general sublime simplicity of the whole. Rocks of grey granite, mixed with portions of a subdued brown, rise all round from the water's edge to the summits of Cruachan and Buachaill Etive, (i.e. the Herdsman of Etive) which last, like a vast pyramid, crowns the whole. The un-apprehended distance lends to these solar tints an atmospheric hue which seems as if it were the local colouring of the scenery, and this brings the entire landscape to one tone of sobriety and broad repose. As no form protrudes, so no colour intrudes itself to break in upon the consistency of the character; even the local colours at our feet partake of the general tranquillity; and all around, water, rock, and hill, and sky, is one broadness of peace and silence, a silence that speaks to the eye and to the mind. The sun shone bright, yet even the sun seemed not to shine : it was as if it had never penetrated to this spot since the beginning of time ; and, if its beams glittered on some grey rock, or silvered the ripple of the shore, or the wild flowers that peeped from beneath their mossy stones, the effect was lost amid the universal hue, as of a northern endless twilight that reigned around."—*Tour in the Western Highlands*, Vol. 2. p. 151.

7. Page 11. " *When now beyond Loch Lurgan, three days thence he reach'd his home.*"

Loch Lurgan, the present Bay of Galway. The residence of Sanchan was in Sligo.

8. Page 13. " *The Coärb of the keys.*"

The successor in an episcopal seat is designated Coärb, as the Coärb of Patrick, Coärb of Columb Kill, &c.

9. Page 16. " *Soar'd and wail'd white Cleena's wave.*"

In the Irish triads,—compositions in the Welsh taste,—the three waves (*tonna*) of Erin are, " the wave of Tuath, and the wave of Cleena, and the fishy-streaming wave of Inver-Rory." The site of the first is supposed to be the great strand of the bay of Dundalk ; that of the wave of Cleena (*cliodhna*) is Glandore Harbour, in the County of Cork. " It emanates from the eastern side of the harbour's entrance, where the cliffs facing the south and south-west are hollowed into caverns, of which Dean Swift has given in his poem, *Carberiæ Rupes*, an accurate though general description. When the wind is north-east, off shore, the waves resounding in these caverns, send forth a deep, loud, hollow, monotonous roar, which in a calm night is peculiarly impressive on the imagination, producing sensations either of melancholy or fear."—O'DONOVAN,

Annals of the Four Masters, A.D. 1557. The wave of Inver Rory is now represented by the "Tonns," which send forth their warning voices in almost all weathers from the strand of Magilligan, near the mouth of the river Bann. The sympathy between the royal shield and the surrounding seas of the kingdom, is one of those original fancies only to be found amongst a primitive and highly poetic people.

10. Page 23. *" Macha, in the ransom-races, girt her gravid loins."*

No more striking instance of the cruelty of savage manners can be conceived than this story of Macha, which is told with much pathetic force and simplicity in a poem in the *Dinnsenchas,* one of the tracts preserved in the Book of Lecan, in the Royal Irish Academy. The *Dinnsenchas* itself is alleged to be, in part at least, a compilation of the Sixth Century.

> One day there came with glowing soul,
>   To the assembly of Conchobar,
>   The gifted man from the eastern wave,
>   Crunn of the flocks, son of Adnoman.
> It was then were brought
>   Two steeds to which I see no equals,
>   Into the race-course, without concealment,
>   At which the king of Uladh then presided.
> Although there were not the peers of these,
>   Upon the plain, of a yoke of steeds,
>   Crunn the rash hairy man said
>   That his wife was fleeter, though then pregnant.
> Detain ye the truthful man,
>   Said Conor the chief of battles,
>   Until his famous wife comes here,
>   To nobly run with my great steeds.
> Let one man go forth to bring her,
>   Said the king of levelled stout spears,

Till she comes from the wavy sea,
 To save the wise-spoken Crunn.
The woman reached without delay,
 The assembly of the greatly wounding chiefs,
 Her two names in the west without question,
 Were Bright Grian and Pure Macha.
Her father was not weak in his house,
 Midir of Bri Leith, son of Celtchar;
 In his mansion in the west
 She was the sun of women-assemblies.
When she had come—in sobbing words,
 She begg'd immediately for respite,
 From the host of assembled clans,
 Until the time of her delivery was past.
The Ultonians gave their plighted word,
 Should she not run—no idle boast—
 That *he* should not have a prosperous reign,
 From the hosts of swords and spears.
Then stript the fleet and silent dame,
 And cast loose her hair around her head,
 And started without terror or fail,
 To join in the race, but not its pleasure.
The steeds were brought to her eastern side,
 To urge them past her in manner like:
 To the Ultonians of accustomed victory,
 The gallant riders were men of kin.
Although the monarch's steeds were swifter
 At all times in the native race,
 The woman was fleeter with no great effort,
 The monarch's steeds were then the slower.
As she reached the final goal,
 And nobly won the ample pledge,
 She brought forth twins without delay,
 Before the hosts of the Red Branch fort.
A son and a daughter together.

* * * * * *

She left a long-abiding curse
On the chiefs of the Red Branch.

* * * * * *

REEVES'S *Ancient Churches of Armagh, App.* p. 42.

11. Page 24. *" Thronging from Dun Dealga bring them."*

Dun-Dealga, giving name to Dundalk, the residence of Cuchullin. There are few better ascertained sites in Irish topography than that of the actual place of abode of this hero. It is the great earthen mound, now called the moat of Castletown, which rises conspicuously over the woods of Lord Roden's demesne, on the left of the traveller leaving Dundalk for the north.

12. Page 27. *" I was head of Rury's race ; Emain was my dwelling-place."*

The petty kings of Uladh (Ulster) who reigned at Emania, claimed to derive their pedigree through Rory More, of the line of Ir, one of the fabled sons of Milesius, as other provincial *Reguli* traced theirs to Eber and Heremon. A list of thirty-one of these occupants of Emania before its destruction, in A.D. 332, compiled from the oldest of the Irish annals, has been published by O'Conor (*Rer. Hib.* SS. vol. ii. p. 66), in which Fergus, son of Leide, the fourteenth in succession from Cimbaeth the founder, has twelve years assigned to him, ending in the year B.C. 31 ; after whom appears Conor, son of Nessa, having a reign of sixty years.

Dr. Reeves, in his learned tract, " The Ancient Churches of Armagh," has collected the native evidences of the early existence of Emania, and of the transition of its original name *Emain,* (appearing as *Hewynna* in 1374, as *Eawayn* in 1524, and *N-awan* in 1633,) into its present corrupt form of " the Navan." The remains, situate in the townland of Navan and parish of

Eglish, about two miles west from Armagh, are now becoming rapidly obliterated. A few years ago, the external circumvallation, enclosing a space of about twelve acres, was complete. Now, through one third of the circuit, the rampart has been levelled into the ditch, and the surface submitted to the plough. Application was made in vain to those who might have stayed the destruction : they could not be induced to believe that any historic monument worth preserving existed in Ireland. Yet a place with a definite history of six hundred years, ending in the Fourth Century of the Christian era, is not easily found elsewhere on this side of the Alps.

13. Page 28. " *The Red Branch House.*"

This appears to have been a detached fortress, in the nature of a military barrack and hospital, depending on the principal fort. The townland of *Creeve Roe*, i.e., " Red Branch," adjoining the Navan on the west, still preserves the name.

14. Page 37. " *O'er Slieve Few.*"

A mountainous district, the name of which is preserved in the baronies of Upper and Lower Fews, on the borders of the counties of Louth and Armagh, the scene of many of the northern bardic romances.

15. Page 39. " *Croghan's host.*"

Rath Croghan, the residence of the *Reguli* of Connaught, erected by Eochaid, father of Maev. Its remains, including stones inscribed in the Ogham character, and apparently of coæval date, exist, two miles north-west of Tulsk, in the county Roscommon.

16. Page 39. " *Binding him in five-fold fetter.*"

This, in the expressive form of the Irish idiom, is termed " the fettering of the five smalls." The quaint translator of Keating

(MS. Lib. R. I. A.) thus describes the performance of a similar operation on Cuchullin by the hero Curoi, from whom he had carried off the beautiful Blanaid : " Chury forthwith pursued him into Mounster, and overtaking them both at Sallchoyde, the two matchless (but of themselves) champions edged of either syde by the stinge of love towards Blanait, and impatient, each, of the competition of a corrival about her, fell to a single combat in her presence, which soe succeeded (as the victory in duells tryed out to a pointe usually falleth out of one side) that Chury, favoured by fortune, and not inferior for valour to any that till that time ever upon equall tearmes mett him, gaining the upperhand of Cuchulluynn, *he bound him upp hand and foote* with such a *perligation* that, trymming of his tresses with his launce (as a marke of his further disgrace and discomfiture) he took Blannait from thence quietly into West Mounster." Elsewhere he uses the forcible expression in reference to the same proceeding—" leaving him so *jugamented,* he went," &c. Of all the translations of Keating this has most of the characteristic simplicity and quaintness of the Irish Herodotus.

17. Page 40. *" On the fair-green of Moy Slaught."*

A very ancient place of assembly among the Pagan Irish, and scene of the worship of their reputed principal idol called Crom Cruach. From the story of Crom's overthrow by Saint Patrick, found in what is called the tripartite life of the saint, it would appear that the stones which represented Crom and his twelve inferior demons were still in situ at the time of the composition of that work, which is said to be of the Sixth Century. " When Patrick saw the idol from the water, which is called *Guthard,* and when he approached near the idol, he raised his arm to lay the staff of Jesus on him, and it did not reach him, he (i. e. *Crom*) bent back from the attempt upon his right side ; for it was to the south his face was : and the

mark of the staff lives (exists) on his left side still, although
the staff did not leave Patrick's hand; and the earth swallowed
the other twelve idols to their heads; and they are in that
condition in commemoration of the miracle :" a pregnant piece
of evidence to show that even at this early time the stone
cromleac, or monumental stone circle, had been disused as a
mode of sepulture: for it is plainly to a monument of that
kind the writer of the tripartite life alludes in this passage.
Dr. O'Donovan has identified the plain of Moy Slaught with
the district around the little modern village of Ballymacgouran,
in the parish of Templeport and county of Cavan.

18. Page 44. *" Practising a constant cast
Daily in secluded leisure, till he reach'd the mark at
last."*

" Oillioll, the last husband that Meauffe had, being killed by
Conall Carnath, she retyred herself to Inish Clothran, an island
lying within Loch Ryve, and afterward used dayly to bath
herself in a well standing neere the entry of the same lake,
and that timeli every morning; and though shee thought her
like washing was secrettly carried (on), yet, it comeing to
the hearing of fforbuidhe vic Conchuvair, he privatly came
to the well, and from ye brym thereof taking by a lynnen
thrid, which for that purpose he carryed with him, the right
measure and length from thence to the other side of that lake
adioneing to Ulster, and carrying that measure with him into
Ulster, and by the same setting forth justly the like distance
of ground, and at either end of that lyne fixing two wooden
stakes, with an apple at the top of one of them, he daily after-
ward made it his constant exercise with his hand-bowe to
shoot at ye apple, till bi continuance he learned his lesson so
perfect, that he never missed his aymed marke; and shortly
afterward, some generall meeting being appointed betweene
them of Ulster and those of Connaght, on the side of the river

Shannon at Innish Clothrain, to be near Meauff, to receive her resolutions to the propositions moved of the other part unto them, fforbuid coming thither with the Ulidians, his countrymen, and watching his opportunity, of a certain morning spyed over ye lake Meauffe bathing of herself, as she formerly accustomed to doo in the same well, and thereupon he, to be spedd of his long-expected gaine, fitting his hand-bowe with a stone, he therewith so assuredly pitched at his mark, that he hitt her right in the forehead, and by that devised sleight instantly killed her, when she little supposed or feared to take leave with the world, having (as formerly is declared) had the power and command of all Connaght 88 years in her owne handes."—KEATING, *O'Kearney's Version, Lib. R. I. A.*

Inis Clothrain, the scene of this shocking treachery, is now known as Quaker's Island. Tradition preserves the place of Maev's assassination, but the well has disappeared.—See *O'Donovan's MS. Collections for the Ordnance Survey of Ireland, Lib. R. I. A.*, vol. " Roscommon."

19. Page 44. *" When he smote the amorous Conor, bowing from his distant stand."*

The late professor O'Curry has fixed with laudable accuracy the locality of this act of savage warfare, at Ardnurchar, i.e., " the height of the cast," in the county of Westmeath. The whole story of the sling-ball, of its nature and materials, of the chance by which it came into Keth's possession, and of the use he made of it, forms a remarkable chapter in the history of barbarian manners.— *Vide* O'CURRY, *Lectures on the MS. Materials of Ancient Irish History*, p. 593.

20. Page 54. *" They turn'd the maledictive stones."*

A pagan practice in use among the Lusitanian as well as the Insular Celts, and of which Dr. O'Donovan records an instance,

among the latter, as late as the year 1836, in the island of Inish-
murray, off the coast of Sligo. Among the places and objects of
reverence included within the pre-christian stone *Cashel*, or cy-
clopean citadel of the island, he mentions the *clocha breca*, i.e.,
the *speckled stones*. " They are round stones of various sizes, and
arranged in such order as that they cannot be easily reckoned,
and, if you believe the natives, they cannot be reckoned at all.
These stones are turned, and, if I understand them rightly,
their order changed by the inhabitants on certain occasions,
when they visit this shrine to *wish* good or evil to their neigh-
bours."—*MS. Collections for Ordnance Survey, Lib. R. I. A.*

21. Page 55. *" Spread not the beds of Brugh for me."*

The principal cemetery of the pagan Irish kings was at
Brugh, which seems to have been situated on the northern
bank of the Boyne. A series of tumuli and sepulchral *cairns*
extends from the neighbourhood of Slane towards Drogheda,
beginning, according to the ancient tract preserved in the
book of Ballymote (Petrie, R. T. Trans, R. I. A. vol. xx.
p. 102), with the *imdae in Dagda*, or " Bed of the Dagda,"
a king of the Tuath de Danaan, supposed, with apparently
good reason, to be the well-known tumulus now called
New Grange. This and the neighbouring cairn of Dowth
appear to be the only Megalithic sepulchres in the west
of Europe distinctly referable to persons whose names are
historically preserved. The carvings which cover the stones
of their chambers and galleries correspond very closely with
those of the Gavrinis tomb near Locmariaker, in Brittany.
The Breton Megalithic monuments appear to belong to a
period long anterior to the Roman Conquest; and this resem-
blance between one of the latest of that group and these *quasi*
pyramids on the Boyne ascribed by Irish historic tradition to
an early ante-christian epoch, goes far to show that a founda-
tion of fact underlies the early history of Ireland.

22. Page 61.   " *to where*
The Danaan Druids sleep."

Irish historic tradition abounds with allusions to the Tuatha-de-Danaans, i.e., the god-tribes of the Danaans, an early race of conquerors from the north of Europe, versed in music and poetry, as well as in the other then reputed arts of civilised life. They are said to have reached the shores of the Baltic from Greece by the same route supposed by the pseudo Orpheus to have been taken by the Argonauts, and by which Homer also seems to have conducted Ulysses. A Greek taste, however derived, is certainly discoverable in the arms and monuments ascribed to this people. Popular mythology regards the race of fairies and demons as of Danaan origin.

23. Page 62. " *When full tides lip the Old Green*
Plain."

The plain of Moynalty, *Magh-n'ealta*, i.e, the plain of the (bird) flocks, is said to have been open and cultivable from the beginning; unlike the other plains which had to be freed from their primæval forests by the early colonists. Hence its appellation of the Old Plain. It extends over the north-eastern part of the county of Dublin, and eastern part of Meath.

24. Page 63. " *A king did on her labour look,*
And she a fairy seem'd."

A liberty has here been taken with the traditionary rights of king Cormac and his wife Eithne, with whose memories the picturesque idyll preserved by Keating ought properly to be associated. The garrulous simplicity of the original is well reflected in the quaint version of O'Kearny.

R

" Eithne Ollaffdha the daughter of Duy.nluing Vic Enna Niad was the mother of Cairebry Leoffiochair, she being the adopted daughter of Buickiodd a remarkable and much spoken off ffearmor (for his great wealth, ability and bountifull disposition of entertaining all sortes of people comeing to his house) who lyved in those dayes in Leinster, and was soe addicted to oppen hospitality that he constantly kept a cauldron in his house still on the fire boyling of meate, both night and day indifferently for all them that came to his house, which doubtlesse by an invitation of that kind procured to bee many.

" This Buickiodd together with his other wealth and substance had seven dayryes of one hundred and forty cowes a peece, with an answerable proportion of horsses, mares, gearrans, and other cattle thereunto; and at length this hospitable and free man was soe played upon in abuseing his plainenesse and liberality by the chieftaines and nobles of Leinster, that they frequenting with their adherents his house, some would take away with them a drove of his kyne, others a great number of his stood mares and gearrans and others a great many of his horses, that, in requital of his free heart, they soe fleeced bare the good man, that they left him only seaven cowes and a bull of all the goods that he ever possessed; and finding himselfe soe ympoverished he, by a night stealth, removed from Dun Boickyodd, where in his prosperity he resided, to a certain wood lying neere Keananas in Meath, accompanyed only with his wife and his said adopted daughter Eithne, and carryed thither his feew heades of cattle. Cormock the king lyving comonly at Keananas in those days, this honest Baickiod for to shelter himself under his wynges and protection, erected a poor cabyn or booly cott for himself his wife and daughter in that wood, where lyvinge a good while in a contented course of life, Eithne did as humbly and diligently serve him and his wife as, if she had been their slave or vassall, their service and attendance could not be with

better care performed, and contynuing in that state, on a day
that Cormock (the king) did ryde abroad alone by himselfe to
take ye aire, and the prospect of the adiacent landes and
valleyes to his said mannor (as he was accustomed for his
pleasure often to do) by chance he saw that beautifull and lovely
damsell Eithne milking of her said ffosterfather's few cowes,
which she performed after this manner. She had two vessells
and with one of them she went over the seven cowes, and filling
the same with the first parte of their milck (as the choysest
parte thereof) she again went over them with the second
vessell, and milked therein their second milck till by that all-
ternate course she drew from them all the milck that they
could yield, the K. all the whyle being ravished with his good
liking of her care and excellent beauty and perfections, be-
holding of her with admiration and astonishment, and she not
neglecting her service for his presence, bringing the milk into
the cabyn where Baickiodd and his wife layd, returns forth
from thence again with two other cleane vessells and a boule
in her hand, and repayring to the water next adioining to the
house she filled one of those vessels with ye water running
next to the bancke of ye ryver and the other with the water
running in the middest of that streame or watercourse, and
brought them both soe filled into the cabyn, and coming forth
the third tyme with a hook in her hand, she began therewith
to cutt ruishes parting (them) still as they fell in her way into
severall bundells the long and short rushes asunder, and Cor-
mock all the while beholding her (as one taken with the
comaunding power and captivity of love) at length asked of
her for whom shee made that selection both of milck, water,
and rushes; whereunto she answered that it was done for one
that shee was bound to tender with better respects if it lay in
her power to perform, and that her performances that way
were but fryday requitalls to the effectual obligation of love
and beholdingnesse wherein she was inviolably bound unto
him, and thereupon the king being both desirous to continue

his further talking with her (such is the wonted effect produced by love and liking when they take any firme footing) and withall willing to finde out whom she soe kindly favoured, asked her what his name was that she soe respected, who answeared that he was Baickiodd Brugh, and the king further questioning her whether he was the same man of that name that in Leinster was famous for his wealth and oppen hospitality, and she telling him that he was the very same man, then replyed the king you are Eithne his adopted daughter. I am sir, said shee. In a good hour sayed the king for you shall be my maryed wife. Nay, sayed Eithne, my disposall lyeth not in mine owne hand, but in my ffosterfather's power and comaund, unto whom they both forthwith repayring, the king expressed his said intention to Baickiod and obtaining his good allowance marryed Eithne and gratified her ffosterfather with a territory of land lying neare Tharragh (Tara) called *Tuaith Othraim* which he held during his life, and that marryage with all requisite solemnityes being celebrated, Eithne afterward bore unto Cormocke a son called Cairebry Lioffachair who grew to be worthily famous and illustrious in his tyme."—*MS. Lib. R. I. A.*

The townland of Dunboyke, near Blessington, in the county of Wicklow, still retains the name of the hospitable Franklin.

25. Page 63. " *The angry Sand-Bull's roar.*"

The sand-banks on either side of the estuary of the Liffey have obtained the names of the North and South Bulls, from the hollow bellowing sound there made by the breakers, in easterly and southerly winds. The North Bull gives name to the adjoining district of Clontarf—*Cluain Tarbh*, i.e. Bull's Meadow,—celebrated for the overthrow of the Danes, A.D. 1014, by the native Irish under king Brian Boru.

26. Page 64. " *The great green rath's ten-acred tomb*
      Lies heavy on his urn."

At this day there is a difficulty in distinguishing the remains
of the Rath of Gavra. It appears to have stood on the slope
between the hill of Tara and the river Boyne on the west.
Several heroes of the name of Oscar perished in the battle of
Gavra. The Ossianic poem which celebrates the battle,
whatever be its age, assigns the rath or earthen fortress as
the grave of Oscar, the son of the bard.

We buried Oscar of the red arms
On the north side of the great Gavra :
Together with Oscar son of Garraidh of the achievements,
And Oscar son of the king of Lochlann.

And him who was not niggardly of gold,
The son of Lughaide the tall warrior :
We dug the cave of his sepulchre,
Very wide as became a king.

The graves of the Oscars, narrow dwellings of clay,
The graves of the sons of Garraidh and Oisin ;
And the whole extent of the great rath
Was the grave of the mighty Oscar of Baoisgne.

                 Transactions Oss. Soc. vol. i. p. 135.

27. Page 67. " *Atharna's lay has perish'd so,*
      Though once," &c.

The story of Atharna is found in the traditional collections
under the title *Ath-cliath*, i.e., Hurdle-ford. It was by him,
and for the use of his flocks, that the ford or weir of wicker-
work was constructed across the Liffey, which anciently gave
name to Dublin. The Leinster people who inhabited the
right bank of the Liffey, resented the invasion of their pas-
tures, and great strifes ensued between their king Mesgedra,

and Conor Mac Nessa king of Ulster, who espoused the cause of Atharna. Mesgedra was ultimately slain by Conall Carnach, who was sent into Leinster in aid of the bardic trespasser : but Atharna's own poetical denunciations were even more terrible to the Leinstermen than the swords of the Red Branch champions. " He continued," says the tract in the Book of Ballymote, " for a full year to satirize the Leinstermen, and bring fatalities upon them; so that neither corn, grass, nor foliage grew for them that year." The miraculous pretensions of the class were continued down to the Fifteenth Century, when Sir John Stanley, Lord Lieutenant of Ireland, was popularly believed to have been despatched within a space of no more than five weeks by an *Aeir* composed against him by Niall " Rimer " O'Higgin, head of a bardic family in Westmeath, whose cattle had been driven by the English of Dublin. See *Annals of the Four Masters*, ad. an. 1414, and HARDIMAN'S *Stat. of Kilk.* 55, n. The plain of Bregia comprised the flat district of Meath, Dublin, Kildare, and Wicklow. In its modern form, Bray, the name is now confined to the well-known watering-place and its fine promontory of Bray Head. *Dun Almon* was, it is said, the residence of Fion, son of Comhal, the Fin Mac Cool of Irish, and Fingal of Scottish tradition. Its name is still preserved in the hill of Allen, and bardic tradition affects to give the name of the builder by whom it was constructed.—O'CURRY, App. 578.

28. Page 74. " *Tirawley, and abroad*
From the Moy to Cuan-an-fod.

That is from the river Moy to Blacksod Haven, in Irish, *Cuan-an-foid-duibh.* The names of the baronies in this part of Mayo and Sligo are taken from the son and grandson of Dathi, the progenitor of the families of O'Dowda. Tir Eera, in Sligo, is so called by a softened pronunciation from Fiăchra, son of Dathi; and Tir-Awley in like manner from Amhalgaid son of Fiăchra.

29. Page 77. " *Was the wind from Barna-na-gee*
o'er Tirawley."

Barna-na-gee, i.e., the gap of the winds, is a pass on the
southern side of Nephin mountain, on the road to Castlebar.

30. Page 79. " *Since William Conquer's days.*"

" William Conquer," i.e, William Fitz Adelm de Burgho,
conqueror of Connaught.

31. Page 83. " *And slew him at Cornassack.*"

" This is still vividly remembered in the country, and the
spot is pointed out where Teaboid Maol Burke was killed by
the Barretts. The recollection of it has been kept alive in
certain verses which were composed on the occasion, of which
the following quatrain is often repeated in the barony of
Tirawley :—

> *Tangadar Baireadaigh,* &c.

> The Barretts of the country came ;
> They perpetrated a deed which was not just ;
> They shed blood which was nobler than wine,
> At the narrow brook of Cornasack."

> O'DONOVAN, *Tr. and Cust. Hy. Fiach.* 338 n.

The territory of the Bac lies over against Nephin mountain,
along the eastern shore of Loch Con between it and the river
Moy.

32. Page 83. " *For an eric upon the Barretts of*
Tirawley."

The eric was the fine for maimings and homicides. When
the first sheriff was sent into Tyrone, O'Neill demanded to

know his *eric* beforehand, in the event, reasonably anticipated, of personal injury befalling him. Singular, that while modern tènderness of human life would abolish the punishment of death in cases of homicide, it ignores the barbarian wisdom which gave compensation to the family of the victim.

33. Page 87. " *'Tis thus the ancient Ollaves of Erin tell," &c.*

The writer has hardly caught the full pathos of that remarkable passage translated below, with which Duald Mac Firbis, the chronicler of Lecan, winds up his account of the retribution thus singularly brought on the descendants of Wattin Barrett. " It was in eric for him (Teaboid Maol Burke) that the Barretts gave up to the Burkes eighteen quaters of land; and the share which Lynott, the adopted father of Teaboid, asked of this eric, was the distribution of the mulct, and the distribution he made of it was, that it should be divided throughout all Tir-Amhalgaidh, in order that the Burkes might be stationed in every part of it as plagues to the Barretts, and to draw the country from them. And thus the Burkes came over the Barretts in Tir-Amhalgaidh, and took nearly the whole of their lands from them ; but at length the Saxon heretics of Oliver Cromwell took it from them all in the year of our Lord 1652 ; so that now there is neither Barrett nor Burke, not to mention the Clan Fiachrach, in possession of any lands there."—O'DONOVAN, *Tr. and Cust. Hy. Fiach.* p. 339.

R3